John Forster

music-lab

a book of sound ideas

Universal Edition

To Dan, Oli,
Tris and Em.

Acknowledgements

I appreciate the help given me quite unwittingly over several years by classes in secondary schools in Birmingham in using material which has found a place here. I am grateful to Antony LeFleming for encouraging work with the Birmingham Schools Training Orchestra and to Robin Whittall and Jill Brown who among other friends have been encouraging and helpful. I owe a special debt to John Paynter for his constructive advice.

ISBN 900938 54 4
UE 26927
Printed in Great Britain by Halstan & Co. Ltd.
Plantation Road, Amersham, Bucks.

CONTENTS

TEACHERS' INTRODUCTION

I hope MUSIC-LAB will stimulate musical experience and help develop musical feeling.

One of the best ways to appreciate a beautiful clay pot is to take a lump of wet clay and use it, play with it, try to shape it, and laugh at your failures. By experiencing the material at first hand your perception will be deepened, and the beautiful clay pot will be seen in a new light. If we encourage our children to become sensitive and alert to sound their whole aural day-to-day existence (from the violin sonata to the ice-cream jingle and the rattle of the cutlery) will gradually have a new perspective. They will begin to appreciate and understand.

As teachers this is our responsibilty. The educational potential of art, creative writing, drama and dance is widely recognised. Music will justifiably retain its dreary crotchet-and-quaver image for children, parents and headteachers until we can demonstrate its force in extending the whole person as a person, and until it can be seen as a compelling influence on the majority of pupils and students, the casual listener as well as the specialist fanatic. If our pupils leave us with a musical awareness we can with some confidence trust them to pursue the varied musical experiences available to them with some intelligence and discernment. Perhaps then we will worry less that they could never remember Haydn's dates or how to notate a major scale. If they leave with a heightened degree of sensitivity and human concern our role in education will have been justified and fulfilled.

Musical skills and technique will be demanded throughout the book but it will matter little whether they are elementary or advanced. Technique alone is useless for it is only a tool. We must become deeply involved in basic musical sound and appreciate its power (emotional, physical, political,...) understand its possibilities, learn how to use it by using it and learn how to make it communicate and express. Much of the work here can be undertaken by positive and imaginative teachers with little formal musical experience. We are, after all, primarily educating people, not programming music machines. If we boast some sensitivity in ourselves we should explore every available channel for encouraging the same asset in our pupils.

This music lab is geared to producing musicians with all the subtlety of meaning that implies. It is not to do with cloning lab rats to fathom the maze of music-related facts and figures. Such information is readily available elsewhere and should be tapped whenever it will raise the level of our students' artistic expression and awareness.

About the book
MUSIC-LAB is written with the general music class in secondary schools in mind. However it could be used in middle schools and also with option groups and general studies groups at upper secondary level. In all cases it is up to you to select and present material in a way which will suit your particular students' maturity, reading ages, musical experience and so on, and use extracts, little or large, to complement other parts of your syllabus.

It is important, too, that students involved in performance ensembles should be encouraged to think and perform 'musically'. Too often school groups are observed performing mechanically to a high standard yet with little feeling or sensitivity. Much of the material here can be used with choirs, bands and orchestras, maybe as a regular warm-up activity at the beginning of a rehearsal. The investment of some time in this way can raise the level of concentration and attainment in the rest of the session.

MUSIC-LAB is not just another book of music projects. Nor is it a step-by-step instruction in music theory. It is not necessary to follow it through from beginning to end although Part One is a gradual and practical introduction to the language of music (not the written language but the things that *make* music a language, speed, texture, balance and so on). The elements are introduced through games and improvisation exercises and some ideas for completely improvised pieces.* In Part Two standard sources of musical

---

*The notational symbols used are explained either alongside a specific piece or in the list on page 72.

sound are discussed and ways of broadening their scope are suggested. These techniques, used increasingly by contemporary composers, can often be acquired by untrained musicians. This does not imply that they should replace or overshadow the normal instruments' sounds or that good standard technique is undesirable. Part Three includes a selection of plans and pieces using approaches and techniques already introduced. The instrumentation is generally left open and performers may incorporate any sounds that are to hand: percussion, vocal and so on. Performers with special skills on orchestral instruments or at the keyboard will be invaluable in extending the scope of the group. The only criterion for fixing instrumentation and for making other modifications to any of the ideas in the book is: 'Does it work, and does it improve the piece?'

Little specific mention has been made of pop music which may be the basis of most students' musical experience and, as such, the point from which our teaching should begin. The aim of this book, however, has been not to make a special emphasis of any particular style but rather to isolate concepts which may apply to any idiom. Most of the work here can well be explored using rhythmic and harmonic idioms and if your class finds these more accessible and acceptable you are encouraged to use them. Wherever your students start, help them to grow both 'vertically' and 'horizontally', increasing both their depth of insight in favourite areas and their general awareness of the rich variety of musical possibility.

Do not overlook the impact of your teaching environment. I doubt that the maximum progress will be achieved from MUSIC-LAB if students are incarcerated in a room designed for another subject or another age. A careful balance of formality and informality, comfort and good playing posture are best for the flow of creative ideas. Arrange desks around the walls leaving a large central area for rehearsal, dramatic work and friendly discussion. Have enough good music stands. Scour jumble sales for rugs, curtains and sofas. Surround your young artists with beautiful things if you want them to feel inclined sensitively to listen, explore and invent.

Related listening and the choice of records

It is refreshing to believe that children can be free to create, unconfined by adult prejudices. Give the child the opportunity and primitive intuition will take over, miracles, perhaps, unselfconsciously emerge. Memory and tradition would smother this freedom as it does each older generation. Yet every great composer has been eclectic in some degree. Even the most original and iconoclastic has a rich background of received music to develop or reject.

The teacher is crucial here. How much should he direct, how much should he wait and encourage and accept? There is no rigid answer. Students' backgrounds and the project being undertaken will point towards the best context to create. However, for all work stimulative input is vital and this will often most helpfully mean listening to other composers' work. Of course we hope to foster originality and self-expression but if our students can sense and handle elements of musical expression as perceptively as professional composers whose work they hear we may be making good progress towards our objectives.

Moreover, many children feel exposed and vulnerable if asked to invent without quite limiting and apparently restrictive reference points, at least at first. Don't be afraid to give them specific and easily applicable models, not to imitate in the way of academic stylistic study but to provide at once an anchor and a launch-pad.

The first draft of MUSIC-LAB tried helpfully to recommend well over a hundred recordings which related to specific projects. Most of them have by now been deleted, such is the speed at which the musical world is changing. New and exciting material is constantly appearing and, while a few references are still included, there is no complete alternative to us, the teachers, listening to a broad and extensive range of music, probably beyond that which we might privately choose, and being alert to any piece which can help us in our classroom task. Use your class listening time actively to generate reaction and invention and introduce music from all centuries, all styles and all countries to enrich your students' understanding and appreciation of the medium we call music.

Science Labs are forward-looking places, bent on discovery and understanding of the physical world. Can we bring some of this excitement to our less tangible field? I hope MUSIC-LAB may help.

PART 1: IDEAS AND INVENTIONS

In the beginning – BANG? (page 15)

New Musicians who are self-conscious have to overcome initial inhibitions before they can become productive. Always be prepared to deviate from the precise line of development taken by the book; encourage a feeling of adventure and exploration. You may wish to suggest work on one of the Creation Story projects in Elizabeth and John Paynter's *The Dance and the Drum* (Universal Edition, 1974).

Textures (page 28)

A colour (scarlet), a texture (gravel path) are rich visual and tactile sensations in themselves even before we use them in a painting or a garden. It is the same with aural sensations; each is full of interest – and then of potential. Look again at the distinctive yellow plastic of your ball-point pen, listen to the sound of the instrument you play or the hum of a crowded room. Are they not part of a rich life-experience, the richer for having looked again?

Many of the assignments here ask for texture building which will involve more than one sound source. Always draw attention to the compatibility of the sounds which are being juxtaposed. To draw a visual analogy again, red, yellow and blue are pleasant enough, but mixed together is the resulting brown satisfactory? So, for example, a 'damped' cymbal or a maraca could both independently give an account of 'network' texture; but put them together and see if they complement each other positively. As a purely musical exercise, work the assignment on page 29 in which 'textures are gradually built up and dismantled', very carefully considering the *compatibility* of the sounds and the *interest value* of the total sound at each stage.

Timbre: the colour of sound (page 30)

In work with non-musical stimuli *('Make weather music', 'Write a tone-poem')* most new composers will naturally choose or try to find appropriate tone-colours, and in such descriptive or evocative music, in film scores especially, we rely heavily on the timbres to help us to the musical sense. Yet we are generally unpracticed in appreciating tone-colours abstractly (not until Ligeti and other modern writers were we asked to), though we are quite at home listening to abstract chord and key progressions and abstract pitch patterns. This chapter encourages concentration on timbre as a source of beauty and as an expressive dimension in itself.

Or is it just a matter of taste? (page 33)

Previous chapters have identified some of the ingredients of musical language. Begin now, by looking at motivic development, to raise the wider issues of unity and balance. How can a piece have interesting variety yet still hang together? Gradually challenge your students to be more perceptive and self-critical. 'Is there too much of that?' 'Have you overdone this feature so that it loses its freshness?' 'Is it good that this section is so much longer than that?' 'I like the way those two ideas contrast with each other' 'Do you think we could use this phrase in even more ways so that we feel the music holding together more, rather than just rambling on aimlessly?'

Basic, factual explanations of 12-tone technique are to be found in most books on twentieth-century music. More detailed information may be found in *Serial Composition*, by Reginald Smith Brindle (Oxford University Press, 1966), or, along with information on many other approaches to composition, in *Twentieth Century Harmony*, by Vincent Persichetti (Faber and Faber, 1961).

But which note is which? (page 34)

If you have worked so far in a free, atonal way melody and harmony can now be introduced as further musical elements alongside dynamics, texture and so on. If you have chosen to use simple diatonic styles in earlier chapters use the material here to extend your students' vocabulary.

In *Twentieth Century Harmony,* Vincent Persichetti explains and offers exercises in writing with scale patterns and techniques similar to those suggested here and usefully supplements each section with references to works by major composers which use each specific technique.

Form is introduced again in the pieces on page 35 and this very unifying ternary shape should be offered and recommended strongly to new composers. If appropriate, related classical forms such as the sonata, *da capo* aria, and by extension rondo and verse and chorus, could also be suggested. Even pieces which have other formal constraints, a piece following a story for example may benefit musically and aesthetically from some reference to opening material.

PART 2: THE APPARATUS

Just as a painter or sculptor may produce pieces which are nothing more than investigations of his medium, the musician must be interested also in the materials he uses. Familiarity with his sound sources will enable him to express himself with greater fluency. Therefore encourage every glimmer of interest which a student shows, even if it is of little 'artistic' value. Allow times for free experimentation, for playing with unusual timbres, extremes of register, clusters and so on, and for playing familiar though mundane cliché-ridden pieces. Allow a short time at the beginning of work sessions for players to establish a familiarity with their instrument, even if it is one which that person frequently plays. No-one attempts the high jump without loosening up first, so we should not expect really constructive and sensitive use of an instrument if the student comes to it 'cold'.

There is no chapter here on percussion equipment. In most schools it is already well used and established and it is likely to be the staple ingredient for practical music making – both creative and recreative – in the classroom. Percussion sounds will inevitably be employed in many of the projects and pieces in MUSIC-LAB and you should encourage a sensitive and exploratory attitude to the potential of the instruments. The work of contemporary composers will provide an endless source of ideas. The following chapters, however, aim to concentrate attention on other, generally less used sound sources to encourage an extension of their use in school music making.

Voices and things (page 43)

For those teaching in a situation with no hardware this may be the place to start your pupils' explorations. Many of the assignments and pieces in Part One are also possible in vocal versions.

Pianos and organs and things (page 44)

Be prepared to encourage even totally untrained performers to use the piano or other keyboard instruments in the course of normal class or group work. The sound is often more immediately impressive than a small pitched percussion instrument and a piano can provide for a whole group (interior/exterior; 2 or 3 at the keyboard), leaving more instruments to go round the remaining groups.

Pop groups are using keyboards more and more with great effect. Remember that in this context one player may be playing only a single lead line *or* a rhythmic chordal backing; seldom both together. Divide roles as far as possible in experimental class/group work too, either with more than one keyboard player (most beginners could easily learn a three chord ostinato) or by using the keyboard to provide only one element in the total sound. It is only when left and right hands are asked to do fundamentally different things that life becomes difficult.

Recorders and things (page 46)

The recorder has a poor image, largely because of its insensitive use as a notation teacher in thirty-strong descant groups. Overcome this prejudice; encourage students to play the recorder, and encourage those who do to move freely from one size to another. The fingering of the descant and tenor are the same, the lowest note being C (they are 'in C'). The others are all in 'in F'; you can still use the same fingering as for the descant but the lowest note (all holes covered) will sound pitch F, not C.

Winds and strings (page 48)

There is a temptation to segregate orchestral instruments from the general class situation. Yet an odd clarinet or elementary french horn or cello (open strings plus out-of-tune effects only for a few weeks maybe) could, apart from teaching factual information about 'instruments of the orchestra', improve a group's impact and potential expressive range a lot.

Do not be reluctant either to encourage conventional ensembles and orchestral groups to work at assignments and pieces from MUSIC-LAB. Apart from offering some relief from the exhausting technical exercise of learning and playing conventional parts accurately it offers great rewards in developing musicianship and musical awareness in our musical specialists.

Players who are reasonably advanced on woodwind instruments should be introduced to the techniques explained by Bruno Bartolozzi in *New Sounds for Woodwind* (Oxford University Press). He gives here many cross-fingerings on each of the four orchestral woodwinds to produce specific multiphonics.

The Concrete path (page 49)

No book encouraging musical self-expression would be complete without reference to electronic media. It is an area which is extensive and quickly changing and detailed work falls outside the scope of this book. On the other hand no school music lab would be complete without it. Much of the work in Parts One and Three can be interpreted electronically and sophisticated, easy-to-use equipment now falls within the financial scope of most music departments.

You may find that students who have been too self-conscious to produce much in ensemble work will prefer the more solitary situation of the electronic studio. This new-found secure environment may enable them to develop both in purely musical terms and in self-confidence. Others may find that manipulating sounds electronically and subjecting them to objective scientific treatment offers satisfaction which other types of musical composition do not. All composers have different interests and different aims in their work; one may prefer to build large impressionist tone-poems while another can only successfully work through tightly-knit fugues or serial canons. As far as we can we must try to match our students with styles and approaches through which they can develop best.

PART 3: BITS AND PIECES

Where precise pitch is important, parts for transposing instruments will need to be rewritten while some pieces could be completely transposed to a new pitch if this enables particular players to take part. All of the pieces are written in Treble Clef since most people learn this initially and there are usually more players of treble than bass instruments. Nevertheless it's hoped bass players will adapt as much of the music as possible. But take care to see that the final effect of several bass instrument players together does not make too thick and muddy a texture. As always the ear is your judge; does your version sound O.K.? With this rule in mind do make any modifications you wish if this enables friends to play together and make a satisfying sound.

Students should be given opportunities to conduct whenever possible (and not only their own compositions). The conductor moulds the piece and his creative role should be experienced just as that of the ensemble member. On the other hand there is no reason why the teacher should not sometimes play the leading role in a piece, perhaps simply to supply a part which others cannot master or, very usefully, performing a 'stimulating' role in anything which depends on improvisation; he won't want to 'take over' the piece, but by offering ideas (musically), developing material and subtly shaping the piece he can draw the other performers onwards to see relationships and make better contributions themselves.

Chorale (page 52)

The instructions in the score are self-explanatory. But inexperienced performers, approaching this as a technically simple piece, may need considerable help with improvising superficially simple textures; are they playing too much, are they playing consciously and imaginatively, placing each sound carefully, or just doodling?

Space-to-fill (page 55)

This score may be taken as the basis for an improvisation by a small group of solo performers. Alternatively a large group, even a full orchestra, can play it with a conductor or conductors cueing groups of instruments and indicating which material to play and perhaps the dynamics, pitch registers and speeds as well. Look at the score / listen to Earle Browne's *Available Forms 2* (Associated Music Publishers, Inc) in which an orchestra is divided into two groups, each with its own conductor and score. The scores are similar to 'SPACE-TO-FILL' in that the range of materials (in *Available Forms 2* each instrument has its own written parts) are printed on one page, and the conductors, responding to the developing sound patterns, indicate which material to play. *Available Forms 1* is similar in many ways but does not divide the orchestra and is moulded by one conductor.

Writers could be encouraged to produce 'available material' scores following Earle Browne's model. Give each block of parts character (as in 'SPACE-TO-FILL') but write accurate pitch and/or rhythm parts. Make a point of contrasting the possibilities offered by each orchestral family; an enormous score sheet might emerge.

Happening (page 59)

This is a piece which can be attempted by players or singers of any technical standard; but it demands performers of considerable aural acuteness and quick reaction. Beginners who try to play 'Happening' will be concerned with simple changes of speed and dynamics. With fluent performers the piece may develop from its restricted opening into a complex improvised piece. The only rule is that every change is stimulated by material already heard. Mistakes, minor fluffing of intonation, accidental *sforzandi*, playing fractionally in front of or behind the beat, are rich areas to scrutinise for slight changes. Acute awareness of what the others are doing, and the ability to put ideas into effect spontaneously are important and valuable musical skills and must be used here to each player's utmost.

Ex-tempo-re (page 60)

Connotations and reflections on aspects of TIME. Individual sections may be worked alone and may stimulate whole pieces from groups or individuals; or the score may be taken in full, as it was originally intended, and methods of performing it as a piece about Time dicussed and agreed. Tape techniques, word-play techniques, recordings of clocks, recordings of material referred to, and so on may all be incorporated into a large-scale sound collage (which could take quite a long time).

Sound around (page 62)

Our visual experiences range from the purely natural (crocodiles) to the purely man-made (bathroom mirrors) and within the man-made from the purely functional ('Bus Stop') to the purely artistic (Picasso). At every level we perceive beauty and ugliness. Moreover we are used to assessing the beauty of man's contribution to our visual world even when its function is not primarily an aesthetic one; we expect our clothes or a new office block to look good and even decorate our food or set out the vegetable garden to look attractive. We are, then, used to being positive in our attitude to visual design beyond the confines of fine art.

We have a duty to encourage our students to be concerned with their aural environment too.

We can see the remains of Roman villages, live in Tudor cottages, and look at Victorian costumes. But the aural environment of the past can only be imagined and deduced from contemporary sources. The tape recorder makes possible a new archive of sounds ('What did a mangle sound like?' 'What can you hear in a non-mechanical society?') which might fascinate and inform a future historian as much as a Gothic throne.

Historical perspectives appear in *The New Soundscape* and *The Music of the Environment*, by R Murray Schafer. It may be possible for some students to attempt similar work on a local scale, concentrating particularly on the last 50 years. Their investigations could include visiting museums, talking to older people, discovering developments in sound-making devices (aircraft, fire engine alarms) and identifying sounds which are now commonplace but would have been unknown a generation ago (photocopiers, liquidisers, Concorde)

A company (page 64)

The solo part here gives an opportunity for someone of slightly greater technical fluency to work at his own level while others cope carefully with the accompanying textures. In a normal class one student may play an orchestral instrument, and this could be supported by a percussion backing. A soloist of very limited skill should be able to manage the solo part with a little practice since each section is based on a limited range of pitches; a beginner may work out possibilities for the improvised 'cadenza' section or even compose and write down his own interlude. This need only be a phrase or two long if that is what he can sustain successfully.

The final section (bar 6) of the accompaniment may be modified to achieve a reasonable sound. As written it implies (part A) a low sustained cluster and (part B) a mid-range cluster, gently moving. Be imaginative; find better ways of using your particular resources to make a calm, drifting close.

After Klee (page 70)

Peter Maxwell Davies's *'Five Klee Pictures'* (Boosey and Hawkes) can be played by a good school orchestra.

It is vital that students are encouraged to *do* and not just expected abstractly to understand. Engage them *actively* as each new idea is explored. Use the bits and pieces in Part 3 and ideas of your own to back up the other work. What you choose will depend on students' skill and your emphasis within each chapter. Here are some possible relationships.

page	Monody 51	Chorale 52	Wizard 53	Wobblate 54	Space-to-fill 55	This way or that 58	Caves 58	Happening 59	Machine 59	Ca-tempo-re 60	Sound around 62	Wind music 63	A company 64	Music; what's the use? 66	Instant coffee 67	The winds will be changeable 68	After Klee 70
In the beginning – BANG?			*					*		*							*
One sound – 3D	*	*				*		*				*					
Movements					*	*		*	*	*			*		*	*	
Sound journeys	*				*	*	*	*		*						*	
Textures		*			*		*		*			*			*	*	*
Timbre: the colour of sound			*	*			*		*		*	*	*				*
Or is it just a matter of taste?		*			*	*			*				*		*	*	
But which note is which?	*			*	*	*	*						*	*		*	*
You are a composer	*		*		*	*	*		*	*	*			*			*
Voices and things	*	*	*	*				*	*	*		*			*		*
Pianos and organs and things		*	*			*		*	*					*	*		*
Recorders and things	*	*		*		*		*				*	*		*	*	*
Winds and strings		*		*	*	*		*	*			*	*	*	*	*	*
The concrete path			*						*	*	*			*	*		*

Part One
Ideas and Inventions

IN THE BEGINNING – BANG?

Do this:

The world, we are told, was created out of chaos. There are more likely scientific theories now, but that was one story worked out by man. And man doesn't like chaos. He likes straight rows and geometric shapes; he likes to be recognisably in fashion (in line) – or out of it. We should all queue for buses, start school promptly at 8.50, wear uniform, eat our soup first and so on. We like to solve puzzles, to see logic and order in everything, remember dates and identify things. We even see faces, mountains and weird animals in the chaotic, random flames of a fire.

The opposite of chaos is order.

The Creation of Man – evolution by natural selection

Perform these pieces :

1.

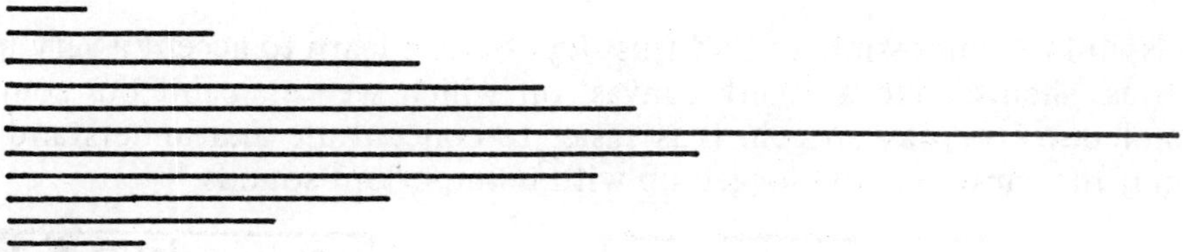

Players start together. Each one chooses a simple repetitive rhythm (on one note or on two or three). Players gradually drop out, which will make both a gradual *diminuendo* and a gradual clearing of the texture, until only one player remains. He continues to play his music. There is no conductor; your ears are your only guides. Listen carefully so that you know when (or if) to stop. Make sure that the sound the group makes changes gently and imperceptibly. No long sustained periods without change; no sudden reductions!

Aim for this 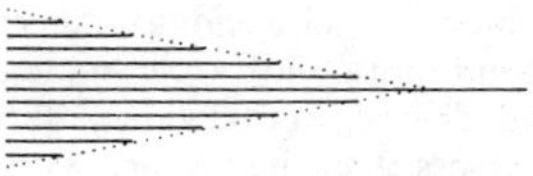 not this 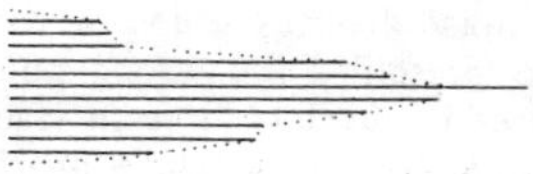

2.

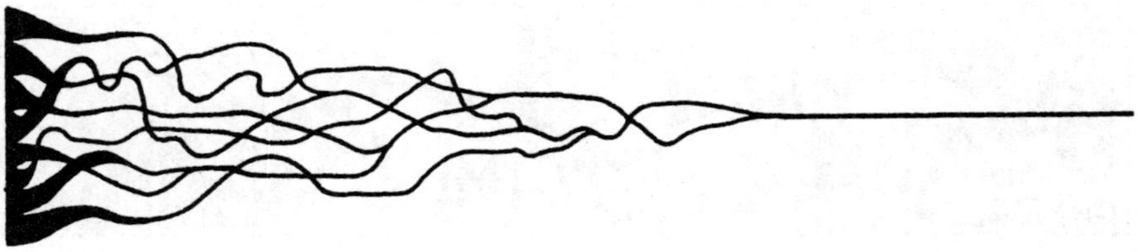

Version a Everyone sings loudly any note to any vowel or word sound (result : big noise). Now, just by listening, gradually change notes to those you can hear others singing until you all eventually (the world took six days!) land on **one** note (not 'fixed' beforehand) singing the **same** vowel or word sound.

Version b The same, but with instruments.

Version c The same but with radios. Agree on a waveband that every radio can pick up. Move the tuning knob to a random position. Switch on; listen; adjust the tuner (and the volume control if necessary) until all the radios find the same frequency (this need not be 'on' a particular station) so that just one sound is heard. Then slowly fade to silence.

The opposite of one sound is random noise.

The opposite of all sound is silence.

Silence is, in fact, impossible to find (just try) but we learn to accept a very low level of noise as 'silence' like a 'blank canvas' on which we can paint our sounds, our music and our everyday speech. It is easier to concentrate and understand what is going on if the canvas is not clogged up with unimportant sounds.*

*Sudden noise disturbs trains of thought (it could cause a road accident, cause you to fail an exam, or your doctor to prescribe the wrong pills). Continuous loud noise not only increases deafness, but also causes disturbances in the bloodstream (factory workers and disco-goers beware!). Workers in noisy foundries have been found to have more family problems and mental illness than the average worker.
What are the laws that control noise? Try to find out. Do thay affect you? Would you like to see changes in these laws?

We are all familiar with this sort of thing: background music; the piped music in supermarkets; in the cinema before curtain-up; in the factory and café, and even in church before the service starts. All these are cover-up sounds, all 'wallpaper music' to set the right mood. They all say that music is unimportant; any soothing rubbish will do.

Let's make one sound fantastically important and listen for that split second when it starts, when it is born. It could be another piece about creation. From eternal blackness life is created; after ages of nonexistance a new thing is born.

Creation Piece 3

. . . s i l e n c e . . .

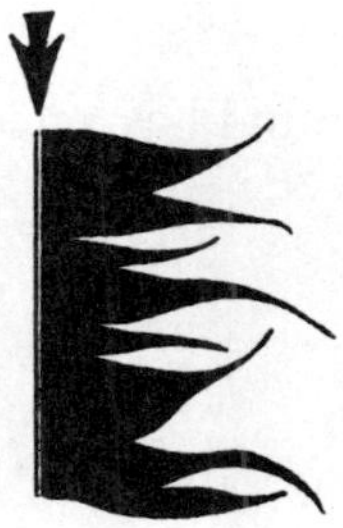

Perform it individually (solo), then in a group with a conductor. Listen to different instruments and voices; see how their sounds all start in quite different ways. You could try it as well, in a group without a conductor, trying to sense – without looking – when other players are about to 'attack'.

Investigate different ways of *attack* (that is, how to *start* the sound) on one instrument.

Find out or make up a theory about how the world came into existence.

Discuss what things were like at each step in the process.

Without using any words use sounds (and silences?) to tell the whole story.

Listen to Darius Milhaud's *La Création du Monde*. What is it that makes it sound so primeval?

ONE NOTE – 3 D

Every sound is 3-Dimensional!

Every sound has DURATION (it's long, short, very long, very short, very very short; or we can be more accurate – half a second long, or a crotchet long)

Every sound has VOLUME (sometimes called *amplitude* – how violently the sound waves disturb the air – or *dynamics*, which means the same, or just *how loud it sounds*)

Every sound has PITCH (it's high, medium, low; it may be a particular note, for example C-sharp, or a known *frequency* vibrating for example 512 times every second)

One note musics

1. Listen to all the instruments available. Can they all produce SUSTAINED sounds (•———)? Do some produce sounds which REVERBERATE after they have been played (•⌒)? Or do some make only very SHORT, *staccato* sounds (•)?

Work out a piece using different LENGTHS of note – and different lengths of silence in between. Keep to one pitch (or one unchanging chord) and don't vary the volume.

For example:

2. Work out a short piece using a continuous note (individually breathing and so on when necessary) Make it interesting only by changes of VOLUME.

For example:

Most music has letters to show degrees of loudness/quietness:

ff	very loud	*mp*	medium soft
f	loud	*p*	soft
mf	medium loud	*pp*	very soft

Find a way of performing this piece; be adventurous.

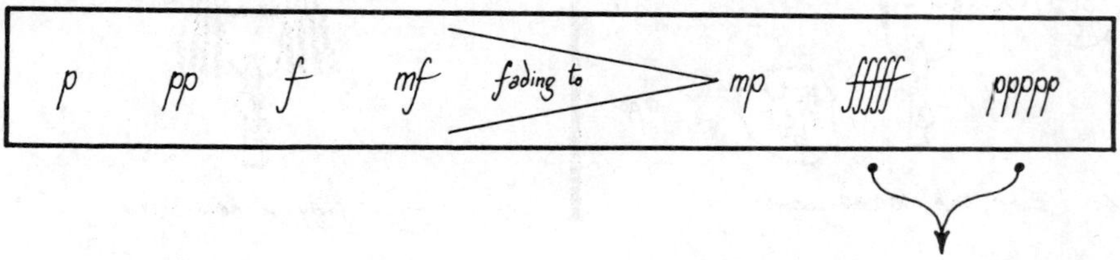

These must be near the limits; the loudest you can bear, the softest you can hear.

A tune at last:

Decide on notes of a particular length and volume. Are they to be played smoothly or detached? Make an interesting PITCH piece.

For example:

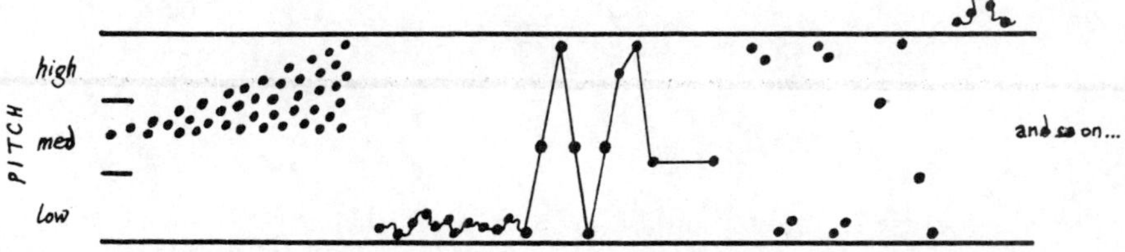

Every sound is 3- Dimensional.

Every sound has pitch, duration and volume, just as every box has height, length and thickness (front to back).

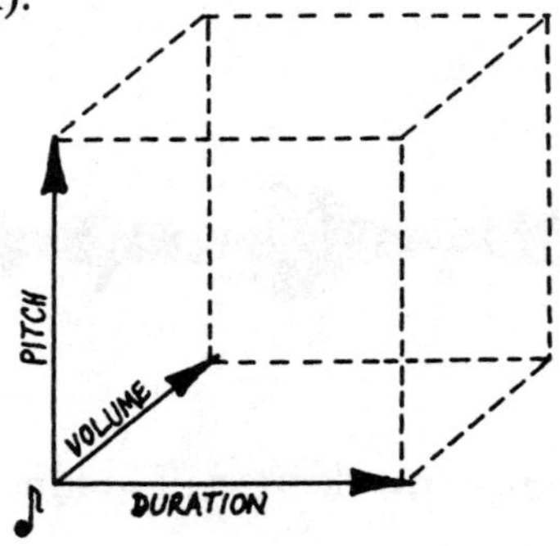

3-D Ping-pong

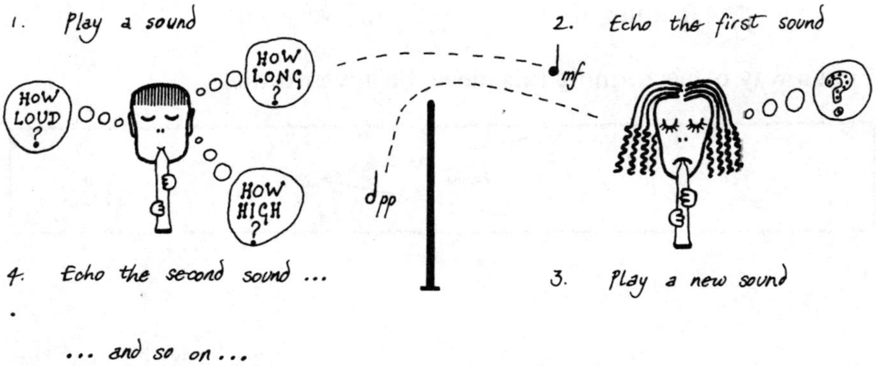

Score points for your opponent's failures.

Next:

Try echoing pairs of sounds

MOVEMENTS

All music has MOMENTUM: a feeling of movement.

Movement is about speed, excitement, urgency — or the lack of these things. Often we find that music has a feeling of momentum because it has rhythm, and perhaps a very strong regular beat. We would recognise it as a fast or slow beat or say that one piece of music moves quickly and another more slowly. This is not scientifically precise. It is what we feel. (We *feel* 50 beats per minute to be 'slow' and 200 beats per minute 'fast'; but compared with 800 a minute 200 is quite slow. Question for discussion: Why do we feel 200 b.p.m. to be 'fast'?)

Sounds can follow each other is simple or complicated ways. The rhythm of sounds sometimes may be very regular. It sometimes needs to be: a military march needs a strict Left-Right-Left-Right. But a general feeling of frantic speed or of gentle rest can be made without a regular beat too. There still may be a rhythm, but not a regular one.

Play these:

1. Man walking

regular beat

2. Man walking — gradually make him run

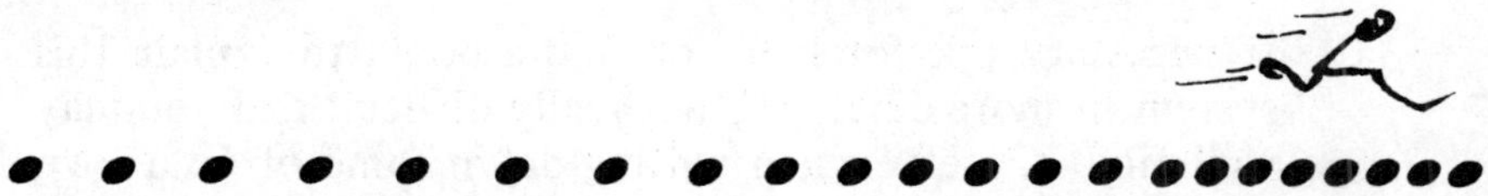

regular beat (slow) — regular beat (speeding up)

3. Beetle looking for breakfast — getting very hungry

no regular beat (slow movement) — gradually faster movement

Both 2. and 3. have changing amounts of momentum – at first slower, then faster. They both have rhythm, but only one has a regular beat. If a piece does have a regular *beat*, that beat can be decorated with a more complicated *rhythm*.

4. Conductor — count steadily 1 2 3 4 5 6 7 8 9 10 11

Player 1 — play

Player 2 — play

Here Player 1 plays a regular beat while Player 2 fits in a more interesting rhythm which nevertheless still 'keeps in time' with the beat. Player 2 can now play his part on his own (counting to himself). He now has an interesting rhythm. (The beat was a boring, unchanging rhythm.)

A drum might play part 1 while a tune is made up using the rhythm of part 2.

It would be possible as well, for each player to use a different beat-speed and not 'keep in time'. The result a different effect! Perhaps more confused, but still interesting to listen to (something like two bands practising in neighbouring rooms).

In traditional notation the piece above would be written like this (well almost; can you spot the mistake?)

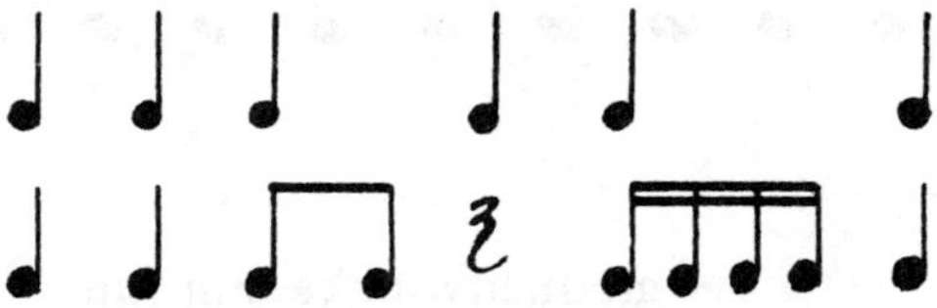

If necessary ask for help, or find a book, to explain this system in more detail. It's not really difficult and you may well find it useful when writing down some of your own pieces later.

Now try this slow music:

5. On a suspended cymbal, use a felt beater (or some other gentle instrument, such as a cello, might be tried).

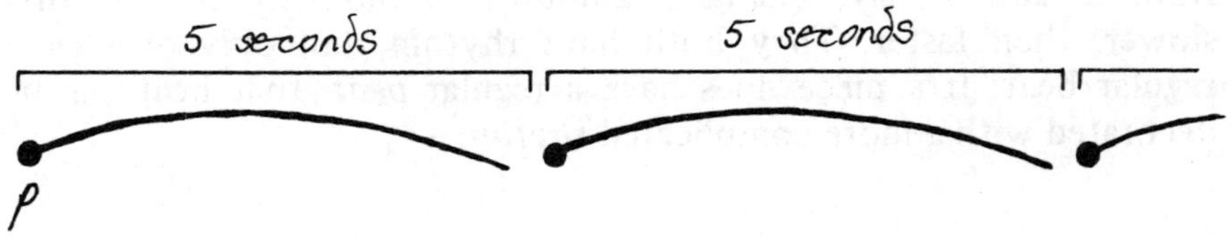

regular

6. Using the same instrument:

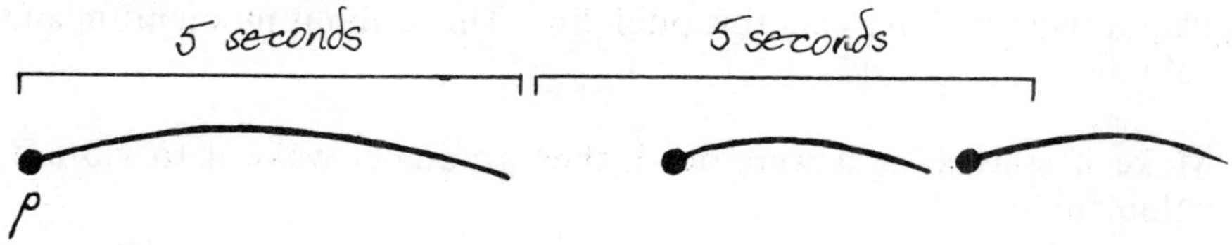

irregular

Momentum does not necessarily depend on rhythm alone, or the speed of the beat, or the time between individual sounds. 5. and 6. both felt relaxed not so much because there was, or was not, a regular beat (in 5. it's so slow it's hardly noticeable), but because the general speed was slow (there were few beats or sounds per minute) – AND BECAUSE OF THE CHOICE OF INSTRUMENT. Both speed and instrumentation gave the piece character.

How does the choice of instrument affect the feeling of momentum?

7. Again on the suspended cymbal (felt beater), cello, and so on, play this:

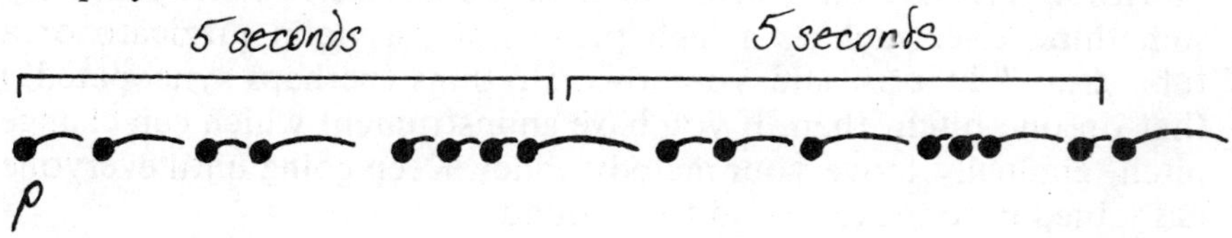

Much faster than 5. and 6. (average about 96 b.p.m.) but still quite a static sound.

Repeat the piece with a wooden beater and make it louder (cello *pizzicato* or *sforzando*). Still relaxed and *still*?

The same speed, yet we *feel* more momentum.

8. Try similar experiments on your own instruments (solo or with others) using only one pitch but different volumes and different ways of attack. Remember your discoveries as you worked 'CREATION PIECE 3' on page 17.

Choose three or four strongly contrasting types of movement; arrange them to make a short piece of music. Perform it to a friendly but critical audience.

Make it important; give it a title.

Play a melody following this pitch line. Think about momentum and volume.

Make it start as if it were dead, then gradually wake it to vibrant, colourful life

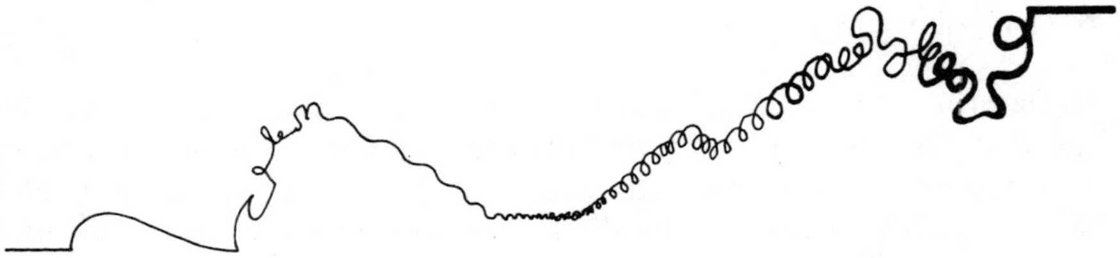

Could it work as a LIFE-TO-DEATH line?

Beats and Backings

Ask one player to keep a strict beat (no speeding up, no slowing down). It may be on a drum or a set of drums, but why not try something else, such as a high piano note, a violin pizzicato or a tuba grunt? In turn add your own rhythms (perhaps syncopated?) first on one pitch, then, if you have an instrument which can change pitch, gradually move your melody wider. Keep going until everyone has joined in to make a good total sound.

Aim for a sound which has a feeling of dance (peasants, children, courtiers, you?). If you feel you are not adding much that is of use, drop out and start again with a new idea. Your piece may look like this:

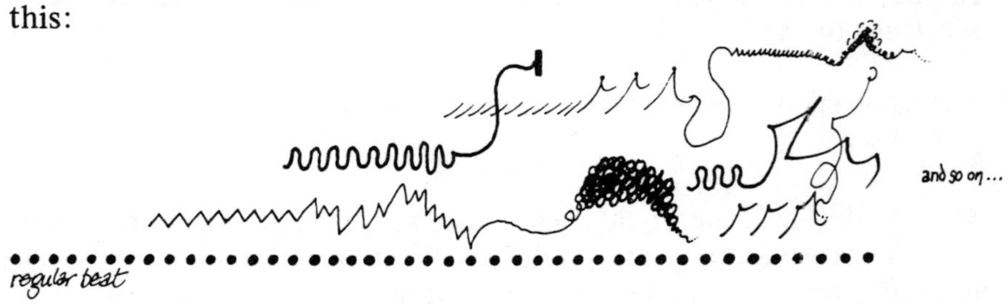

If it sounds too complicated or confused there may be too many people taking part, or maybe they are just not listening and thinking carefully enough. But you could decide that people should play very simple repetitive patterns *(ostinati)* against which you can have solo spots in turn, one or two at a time:

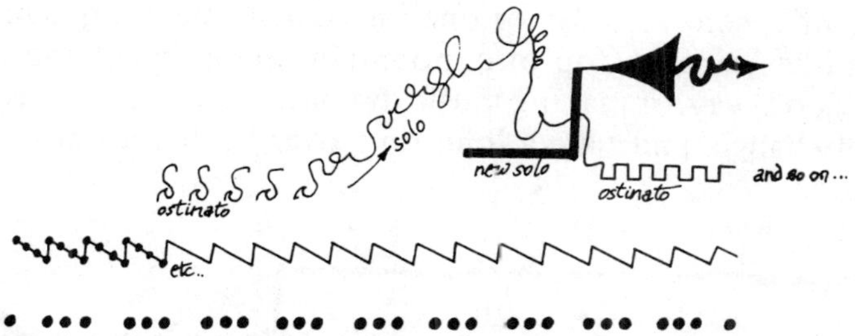

A different effect would be made if the background beat were replaced by a continuous sound, such as a 'drone' (e.g. on a cello  or three flutes  or two voices 

). Folk dancers in many countries use a drone, sometimes with a drum beat, sometimes without. Try it.

Occasionally change the drone slightly, add a beat, cut them out completely or make them loud so they drown everything else, and so on.

Listen to lots of jazz. Try to find out about different types, Trad, Big-band, Modern, etc. Although much jazz is partly or totally improvised – made up as it goes along – there will be features which hold it together. Look out for the strong beat (is there one?), riffs, recurring melodies, and the give-and-take between instruments. Is it based on a simple tune? Does it have a particular mood? Are some solo spots more effective than others? Why? What feeling of momentum does it have? How is this feeling of momentum achieved? Try to draw sections in the way used in 'Beats and Backings', above. Be as accurate as you can by listening as carefully as you can.

A piece using only drones and/or *ostinati*!

Perform it in public.

At times music is full of sudden contrasts; maybe a loud *tutti* chord followed by a soft, gentle, solo melody, or one instrument may stop suddenly and another begin. This is like being on top of a mountain one moment and on the sea shore the next. It is a good way of making music dramatic. But sometimes composers prefer a more gradual change, and take a long time over it, like a long cycle ride from the hills to the sea.

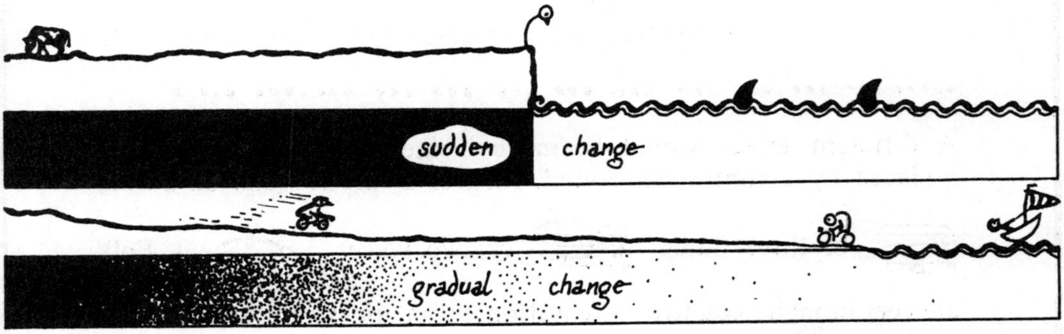

The nineteenth century is usually considered to be the time when music became very dramatic (Mendelssohn's overtures, Berlioz's symphonies, Wagner's operas); instruments became stronger and could make bigger sounds. But the composers of the seventeenth and early eighteenth centuries (Gabrieli, Bach, Monteverdi) were dramatic in their own way. The instruments they had such as the clavichord, recorder and lute, could not increase or decrease much in volume, so changes of volume were made by adding or subtracting instruments; a solo recorder may have been followed by a string orchestra, or many violins reduced to just one or two (Organs and harpsichords worked in the same way; by pulling out more stops, more pipes or strings were brought into play, which had the effect of adding another group of instruments.)

19th century

17th century

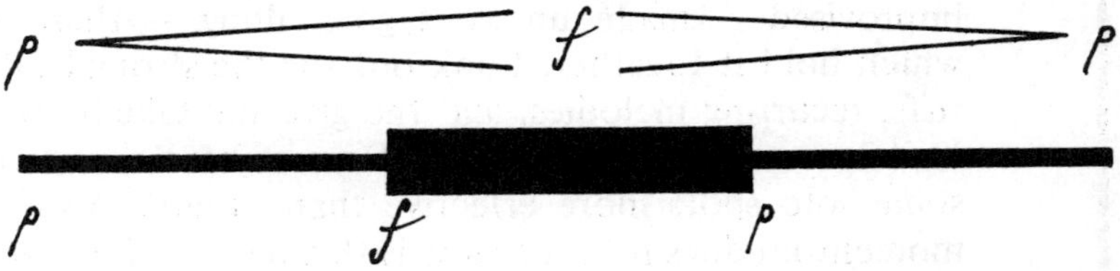

In large-scale impressive pieces *f* followed by *p* would sometimes be achieved by an echo effect made by a choir, perhaps, in some distant gallery.

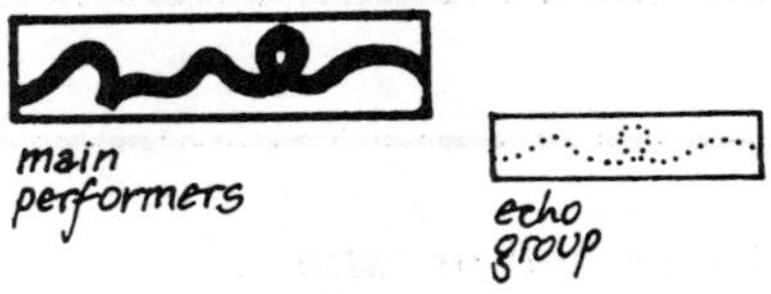

We can learn from all of these methods and make use of any of them. We have the added possibility of changing volume by electronic amplification. A single voice can ring through a stadium, a huge band on record can be made hardly audible and very private.

Think of all the contrasts of sound that are possible.

HIGH ⟵	PITCH	⟶ LOW
SOFT ⟵	VOLUME	⟶ LOUD
LONG ⟵	DURATION	⟶ SHORT
FAST ⟵	SPEED	⟶ SLOW
ROUGH ⟵	TIMBRE	⟶ SMOOTH
THICK ⟵	TEXTURE	⟶ THIN

and so on . . .

Sound journeys

Take one pitch from SOFT —— *to* ——→ LOUD

Take one pitch from FAST — *to* — SLOW — *to* —→ VERY SLOW

Take a few short sounds from HIGH —— *to* ——→ LOW

Take one pitch simultaneously from { SOFT —— *to* —→ LOUD / FAST —— *to* —→ SLOW }

Using the words at the top of the page make up your own sound journeys.

Trio

Divide into three groups. Each group appoints a leader/conductor and then agrees on signs he will use to indicate LOUD, SOFT, GET LOUDER, HIGH, LOW, ROUGH, SMOOTH, WOBBLY, and so on (as many possibilities as you can all easily remember). It may be that each group chooses different types of sounds (brass, vocal, metal, guitars, and so on) but it would be more testing of your imagination if everyone had similar instruments (for example, all chime bars, all kazoos, all humming, all tin cans). Separate the groups. Each conductor follows this score, showing his group through the agreed signs what they are to do. The only rule is that the sounds his group make must contrast in every possible way (in every dimension) with those being made or recently made by the other groups. Each section can go on for as long as the conductor wants, and the sounds within a section can change as well, sometimes dramatically, sometimes imperceptibly.

TEXTURES

A gravel path, a cotton sheet and a playground slide all *feel* different. Their surfaces all have different textures; rough, smooth, soft, hard, boring, interesting, comfortable, painful, ...

In a group, think of ways of making musical textures. Use all the possible ways of making sounds with your instrument. Use the boxes to give you ideas. With your group make each texture in turn.

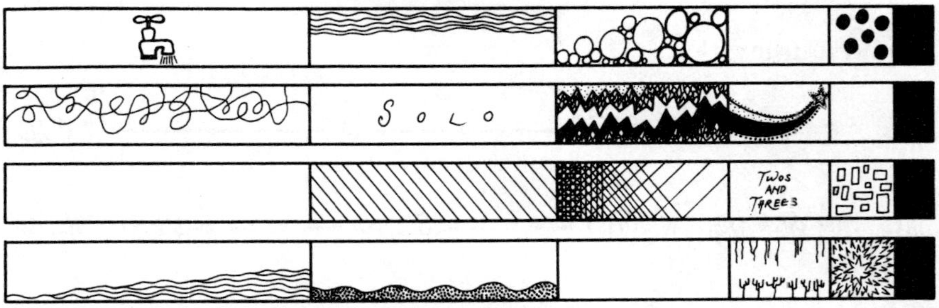

Decide on a route and play through certain boxes. You may decide beforehand how long you will spend on each texture. This is a 'Texture Journey'. Imagine walking through a pitch dark room full of 'feely' textures. You may like to build such a room to play your texture pieces in.

Divide your group into parts (smaller groups) and read the box drawings as a score, either two lines at a time or all four lines together. You will now have to take great care over *balance*; are you playing too loudly or too softly to blend in, or to contrast with the rest in the way you think best? Sometimes have a conductor to each part; sometimes ask one person to conduct the whole sound. At other times work through without any conductor but listen very hard so the balance is right. And make sure it's 'musical'.

How many of these texture boxes could you play well on your own?

Try to work out a 'Gravel Path Texture', a 'Cotton Sheet Texture', a 'Playground Slide Texture'. These are *sound pictures*; they are a good way to start composing. Try suggesting

The skeleton of a dead leaf
Glass marbles
A baby's skin (go and find out)

An old man's skin (go and find out)
Network
Rust
Paper
Fishes' scales
Mud . . . . .

A piece in which textures are gradually built up and dismantled!

Experiment with 'speaking-voice-textures'. You could use a text.

Listen to music which pictures things in sound, such as:

Debussy: *Piano preludes*

The Sea – Britten: 'Four Sea Interludes'

Debussy: *La Mer*

Mendelssohn: ' Fingal's Cave'

Animals – Saint-Saëns: *Carnival of the Animals*

Prokofiev: *Peter and the Wolf*

Bartók: *From the Diary of a Fly*

Listen to music which relies mainly on changes of texture for its interest, such as:

Pendercki: *Threnody: To the victims of Hiroshima*

Ligeti: *Volumina*

Varèse: *Arcana*

Stockhausen: *Carré*

TIMBRE: THE COLOUR OF SOUND

When you listen to an orchestra on the radio you can be sure which instrument is playing although you cannot see it. A trumpet, a xylophone, a singer, and a treble recorder all play  and you know which is which. They all play C, but the 'colour' of trumpet C is different from the 'colour' of recorder C. We know the timbre of our friends' voices in the same way. The Prime Minister sounds different from Bob Dylan or the Queen.

Most instruments can produce many colours or timbres.

Play this rhythm three times:

1. on a low note, played in the usual way;
2. in an unusual way, with a mute, blocked sound holes, with unusual beater (fingers?), etc. depending on your instrument;
3. or use just the mouthpiece, tap the body of the instrument, stroke the strings, and so on.

The same rhythm but different *sound colours.*

Find as many sounds on your particular instrument (or voice) as you can.

Make a catalogue of them in order of beauty.

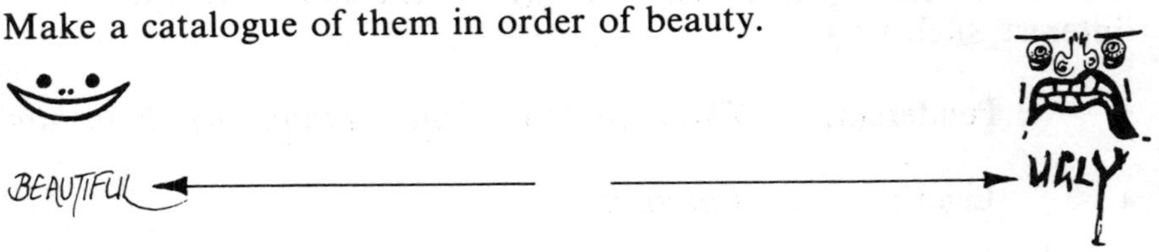

What is it that makes a sound beautiful or ugly?

If you have a gentle, sweet instrument make it sound ugly. If you have a hard, strident, rough-sounding instrument make it sound sweet and gentle.

Could this be the basis of a humorous piece?

Changing colours

Make a piece without rhythm, volume or pitch change.

Pitch: it may be yet another one-note piece, or a piece which keeps the same *chord* (group of notes) throughout; it could be a simple *triad*, e.g. F.A.C.  ; or a *cluster*, e.g. all play any note between E and A  ; or a more complicated chord chosen at random – 'all play any note you wish, and hold it'. (In very sustained music it may be necessary to breath or bow the string again from time to time. If you do this carefully and don't *attack* the new note it will hardly be noticed.)

Give the piece a very subtle, elusive interest by making the timbres change gradually. The colour of the day, from early dawn to dead of night, change imperceptibly slowly.

For example:

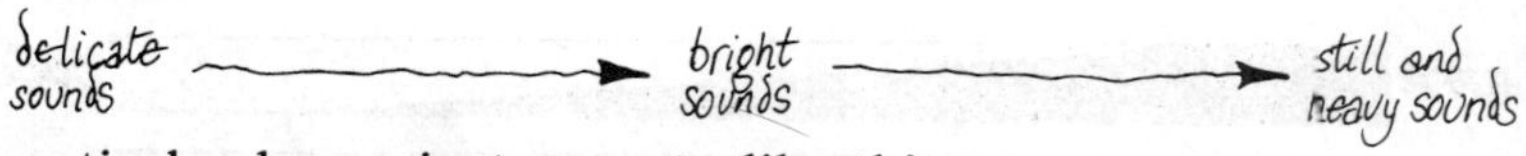

Alternatively change instruments, like this:

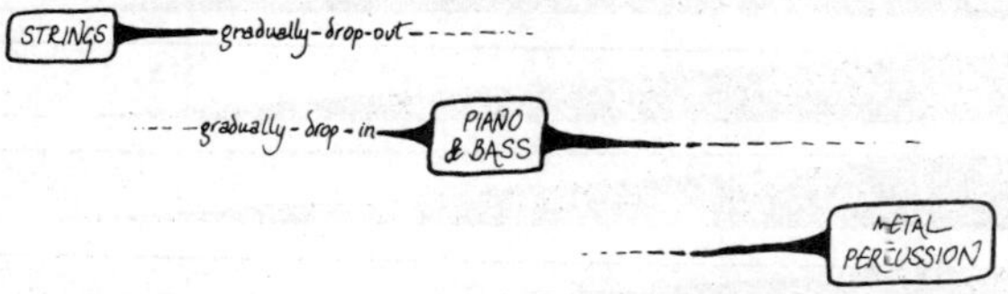

A more complicated version would be to add a chord plan so that the actual pitches changed slowly (everyone moving on to his note in the next chord at his own time so the change of chord would be gradual, clouded). The change of colour would be more pronounced if the chords were very different, as in example 2:

1. 

2, 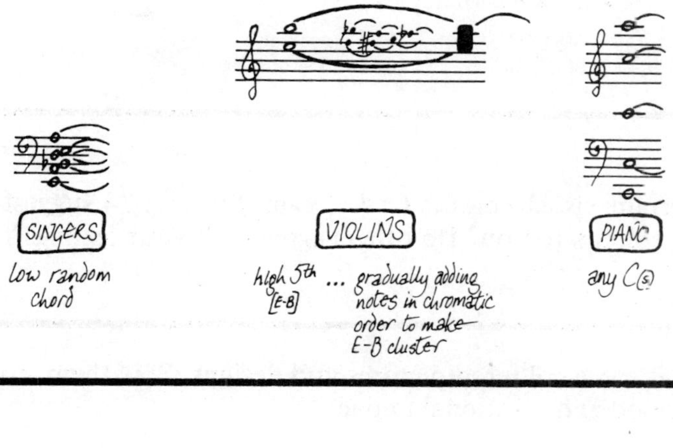

Versions for voices

The timbre of your voice changes with the sounds you make. For instance, the different vowel sounds sound different because you change the sizes of the cavities in your head and throat. Each vowel has two frequencies or pitches and it is the relationship between them which gives the sound its character (rather like the two sounds G and D played together produce quite a different *type* of sound than G and A-flat together).

1. All sing:

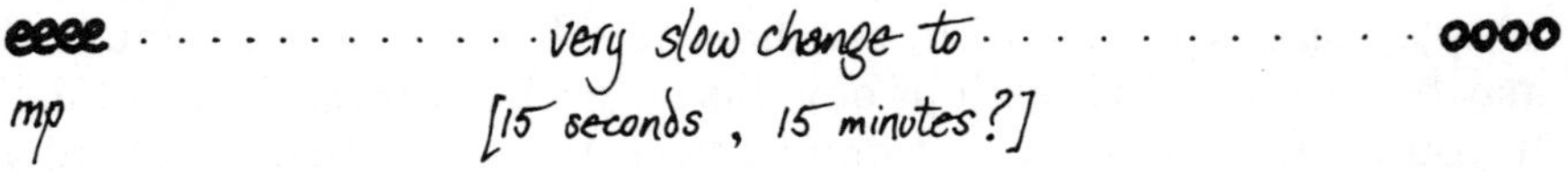

2. Ten singers: The first group (1-5) sing their sounds and hold them, but as they get quieter and fade away, the opposite singers (6-10) 'fade in' their new sounds so the overall volume stays the same throughout.

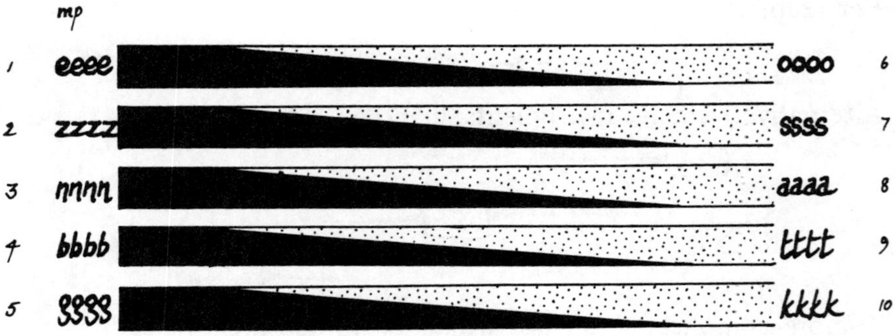

3. Around the room (sit in a circle, or a straight line), change from 'oooo' to 'eeee', but one singer at a time takes the process of change a little further than his neighbour.

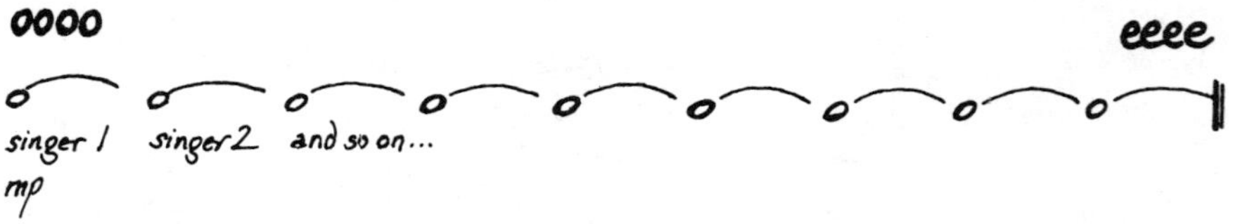

Do certain visual colours (red, cream, lime, . . .) suggest particular sound colours to you? Do others agree with your feelings?

Look at some coloured pictures and designs. Play them, conjuring up their mood and emotional impact.

OR IS IT JUST A MATTER OF TASTE?

We must always think carefully about how much we should change things, and about how much contrast and variation we need. Remember how many ways of making contrast and variety we have already discussed!

A hundred tubular table legs may be boring, while a centipede is always fascinating. But consider the very fantastic reflections in those shiny table legs! So is it just a matter of taste?

We need some variation to avoid boredom, but too much would be restless and disturbing. We may use it to produce a special effect but we usually prefer balance.

NOT TOO DIFFERENT – NOT TOO SIMILAR

Not too different, not too similar, often means that one musical idea will be 'related' in some way to another. A 'Theme with Variations' is the most obvious instance of this but almost every piece of music uses relationships in some way.

How many ways can this simple tune be varied but still remain a recognisable relation?

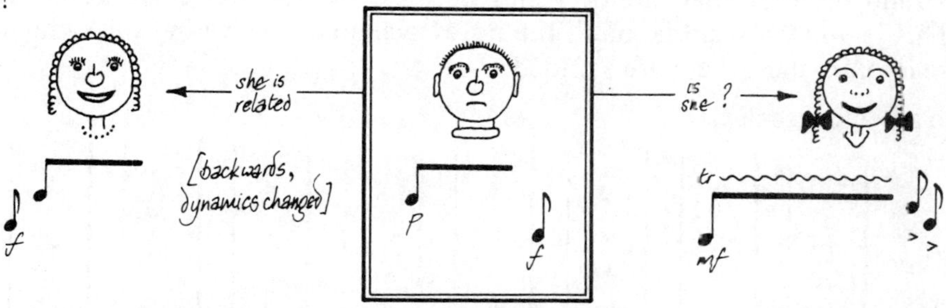

Make a whole piece based on this little phrase. 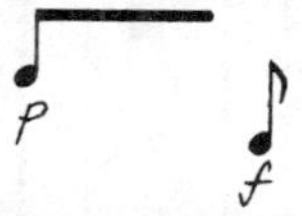

Find out about Schoenberg's twelve-tone, serial technique which uses simple material upside down, backward, and so on to make interesting variations. Listen to music by Schoenberg, Webern and Krenek. Some later composers took serial ideas further to fix dynamics, timbre, rhythm and tempo as well as pitch. Try to hear Babbitt: *Three compositions for piano* (1948), Boulez: *Modes of Time-values and Intensities* (1949), Stockhausen: the very early electronic piece, *Studie I* (1953); *Gruppen* (1955-57) or other pieces by these composers written around the same time.

Try writing simple pieces using Schoenberg's twelve-tone system. Don't forget to play them too. Otherwise they will just remain dots on music paper.

BUT WHICH NOTE IS WHICH?

Early caveman's music probably had a 'tune' of some sort. So has most music since then. Yet you have come this far with your music without having to think much about particular notes, about which note is which.

Until now it has not mattered too much exactly which notes you have chosen to play. You will have chosen your notes with care but all of them have been allowed. You will have tried to understand what gives a piece of music character by learning to use momentum, dynamics, texture, and so on. Until early in the present century this would not have worked; there were always very strict rules about which notes would sound right when played together in a tune or in a chord. But in much of the music that composers have written since the 1920s any note (pitch) can be played with any other. We have become used to this, although our grandparents' parents would have hated it and called it discordant and wrong.

This does not mean that notes or exact pitches are now unimportant. It means that other elements can also be used to create the piece that the composer has in mind. Elements such as timbre, can give a piece its character and interest. When you decide to use a particular set of notes (a scale, a chord, and so on) you have another technique which will determine the character of your music. You may know that major scales sound brighter than minor scales because of the particular notes which are used. This is what a scale is; of all the notes available (twelve in each octave) certain ones are chosen and others are avoided.

Here are a few scales:

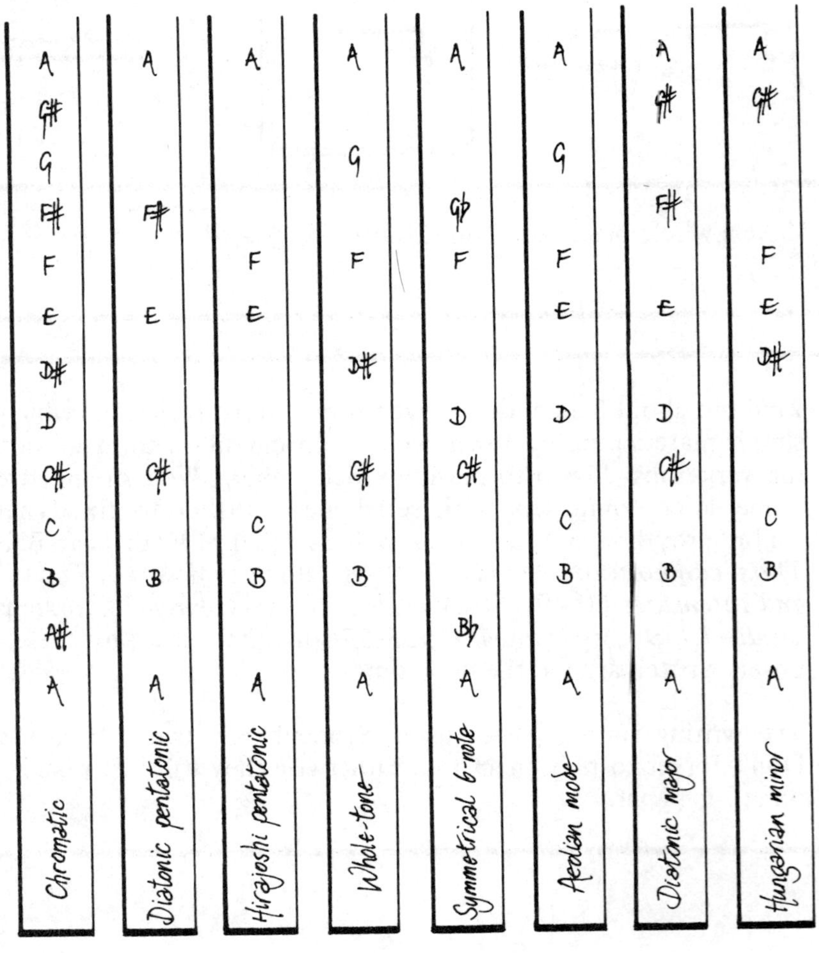

However you could well start your experiments with much smaller and simpler scales.

Piece A

Choose any three pitches. You are allowed only these notes (though at any octave). Make up a small group piece. You could include a 'singing line'. Is your scale easily singable? Do you feel that one particular note feels stronger than the others and wants to be the finishing note? It often happens in scales, unless every interval – distance between notes – is identical. Which of the scales above has every interval the same?

Piece B

Make a contrasting piece using a different, or partly different group of notes. How much should it contrast? Should it keep *some* features the same?

Fit these two pieces together to make a longer piece, repeating Piece A at the end:

Piece A . . . Piece B . . . Piece A again.

This is a useful plan to use frequently. It appeared in early folk music and has been popular in nearly every period and style since. It is called 'ternary form' and is sometimes compared with a bridge or arch, where two similar pillars support a different centre:

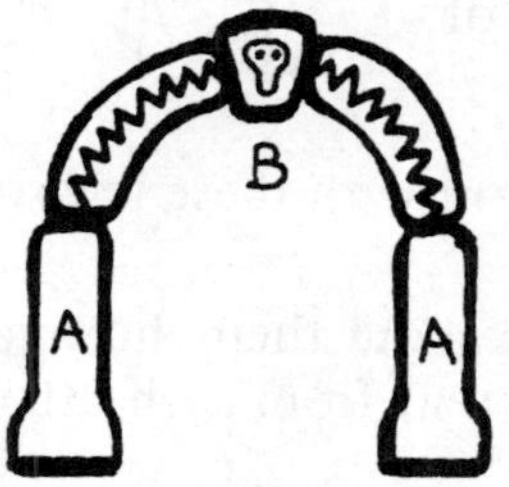

There need not always be a distinct break between Music A and Music B:

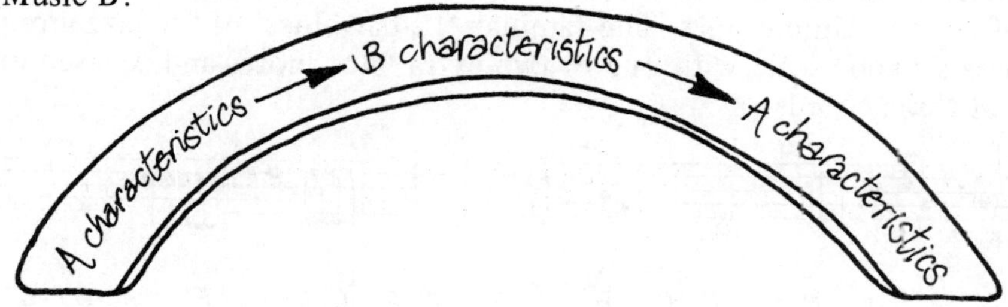

Cutting our scale down to two, three or four notes, we begin to feel we are working with a chord in which all notes sound happy when played together. (All the notes of the diatonic pentatonic scale (page 34) sound pleasant together, which makes it a useful scale for improvisation work.)

A simple chord is generally made up of three or four notes, though chords can easily use more, or even all twelve notes of the chromatic scale. They are usually selected from the scale in use by various rules. Many common chords are built by *thirds* but other intervals can be used to produce a different sort of sound, with a different character.

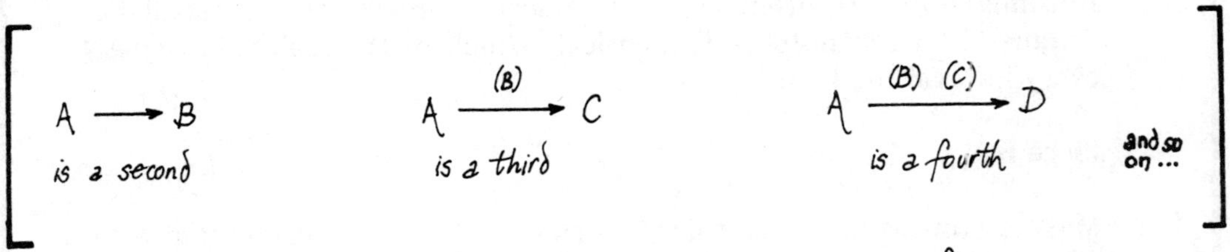

a chord built on thirds

a chord built on seconds

a chord built on fifths

a chord using a mixture of seconds and sixths

You may find it fun to experiment with these ideas.

You may want to find out more about them; how various composers have used them and how their music sound different from each other's.

Many songs and pieces we know use scales and chords, and these are often very simple ones. The familiar '12-bar blues' of the jazz group uses a major scale with one or two extra 'blue' notes and is based on just three chords:

Repeat this over and over again altering the tune each time, but always drawing mainly from the notes available in the chord. As you become more confident and used to making up these tunes try decorating the basic chords by using other notes of the scale (like the D in bar 5) or even foreign notes; on these chords experiment first with E♭, A♭, and B♭. Try different speeds and rhythms; make pieces build up, calm down and change in other ways, so that they have an interesting shape (form).

Try working out a simple chord sequence (not necessarily with thirds chords) and repeating it. It becomes an *ostinato.* Weave more interesting tunes over it. They could have a regular rhythm but do not have to.

1. In the tune, use just the notes of the chord in use. For example:

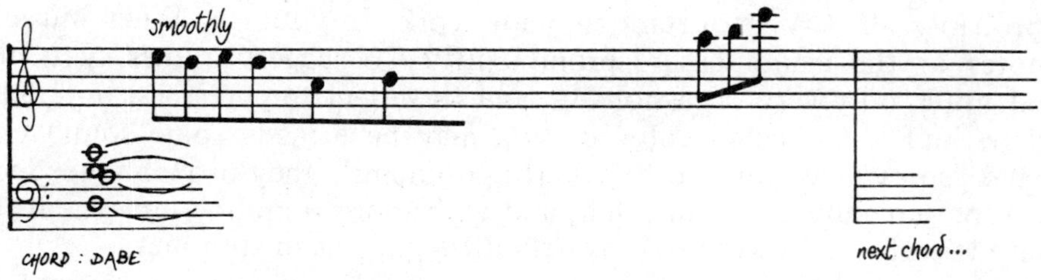

2. Be more adventurous. Use some foreign notes:

3. Use any pitches; give the tune character in other ways:

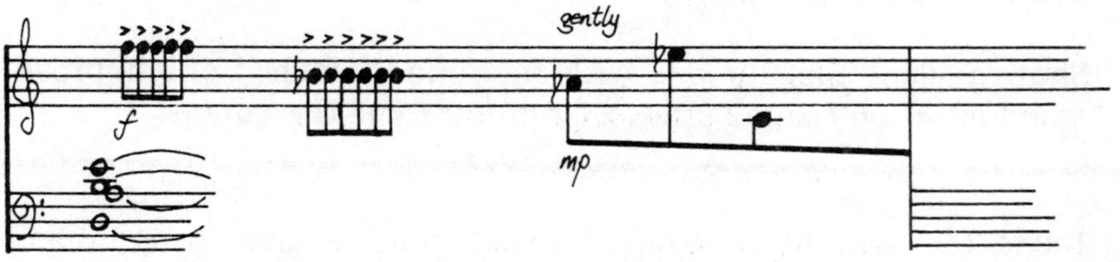

After working through these experiments you may feel that scales and chords are useful in working out the sort of music you want to write, or that you like the restrictions they make for you. Many composers do. Or you may just want to keep the ideas in the back of your mind to use at the right time, and feel that for you, other elements are more important.

YOU ARE A COMPOSER . . .

. . . commissioned to write background music for a film. The scene is motionless; icicles hang from a frozen ledge; you can feel the crisp, freezing air, you can see the hard-packed snow glistening in the early morning sun. The impoverished film company can only afford a piano. Find piano sounds to match that scene. Experiment and decide what you find most satisfying and convincing.

Now try another scene. This time two heavy hippopotami are wallowing in a deep muddy river doing their best to frolic like lambs (which they saw on a recent safari to the Cotswolds) . . . . Think about it, then try out various ideas.

You have just composed some music. TONE-COLOUR, RHYTHM, and MELODIC STYLE were probably all very important in your work. In your 'Icy Dawn Music' did the high notes of the piano feature prominently? To suggest stillness you may have changed notes only very occassionally, and to reflect the crispness and delicacy of the icicles and hoar-frosted cobwebs you may have made some sound extremely short and 'spiky'. As for the 'Potty Hippopotami', they probably needed sounds which were generally lower in pitch, and with more rumbling movement, and you may have tried to find ways of doing ugly little jumps and stumbles.

You have considered the types of sounds you needed, which part of the piano (high, low, keyboard, interior, case) would suit you best, whether there should be much movement and excitement, and how loud it should all be. You have made decisions about exact rhythms and pitches knowing the timbres available from the piano. Gradually everything falls into place and the best solutions are decided upon. Imagine your 'Hippopotamusic' played on a glockenspiel or a violin. Would it still work?

Make one of the films. Keep it short but good. It could be a cartoon. Or a slide show with music.

Show a silent film, or one with the sound switched off. Improvise mood music and sound effects. Or do the same for a mime.

Having found the right tone-colours, thought must be given to PITCH and RHYTHM (is the music to be wide-leaping or smooth, static or with great urgency?) and FORM (the shape of the piece, how the music might develop, whether sections might be repeated, and so on). The title or original idea or story-line may suggest a plan to work to. When composing, careful planning is important. Have possibilities in mind, jot down a framework even if it is changed as you work through the piece.

A composer usually writes down his ideas, so he can remember his music and others can learn to play it. He may also want to look back and make alterations or corrections later. If you want to write your music down, don't be afraid to invent your own simple memory-signs if you are not sure how to write it in normal music notation.

There are several ways of starting a piece.

One way is to start with a master plan.

Choose a title or theme:

- the film topics already mentioned
- geometric shapes
- contrasting textures
- swimming
- growing anger
- buildings
- glass
- recent news

Begin by looking at a picture or scene:

- find paintings by Mondrian, Klee, Matisse, Miró
- or by Breughel, Canaletto, Turner, da Vinci
- the sculpture in your school or shopping precinct
- the cover of this book
- a painting or sculpture of your own

Choose a story or favourite poem.

Begin with a musical idea:

- a very long and interesting crescendo
- variations on a theme
- duet
- a round, a rondo, a retrograde rhythm

Discuss your ideas and try out small sections. Criticise each other and keep improving the overall sound. Record your work and judge it for yourself. Eventually you will have made 'a piece of music'. Composing is not just for a few musical geniuses.

Not all music needs to be written down. IMPROVISING (making up a piece as you play it) is good fun and a very useful musical activity, especially in a small group of friends. It is also hard work. Once you have made the first sound in a piece there is no going back, no rubbing it out; the rest must fit and follow naturally. Every ounce of concentration will be needed to think ahead, to think back to what has already been played and consider in every detail what to play at every moment on the way.

Group improvisation is very similar to 'musical conversation'. Each person puts his own point of view, listens, agrees, disagrees. But remember in a sensible conversation no one speaks all the time; if everyone makes selfish comments without listening to the others the result will be Bedlam. Musicians call it cacophony.

This is another good way of working which will help you develop your 'MUSICAL SENSE' if you can listen hard enough.

Begin with a solo phrase ::: Someone else plays an answering phrase ::: Was it good?

A longer piece of music is really an extension of this idea. A tune or texture comes along and is answered by others, sometimes blending in, sometimes contrasting. At times it can involve a few players and at other times everyone can add their voices.

You must now, more than ever, keep an ear for the overall sound in which you are taking part, and be aware of as much minute detail as possible in the other players' musical ideas. Otherwise, how can you reply to them sensibly? What *was* the last note your neighbour played? What *was* the interval the player opposite used?

Here are some simple opening phrases on which simple games or more elaborate improvisations could be based. Invent your own openings too.*

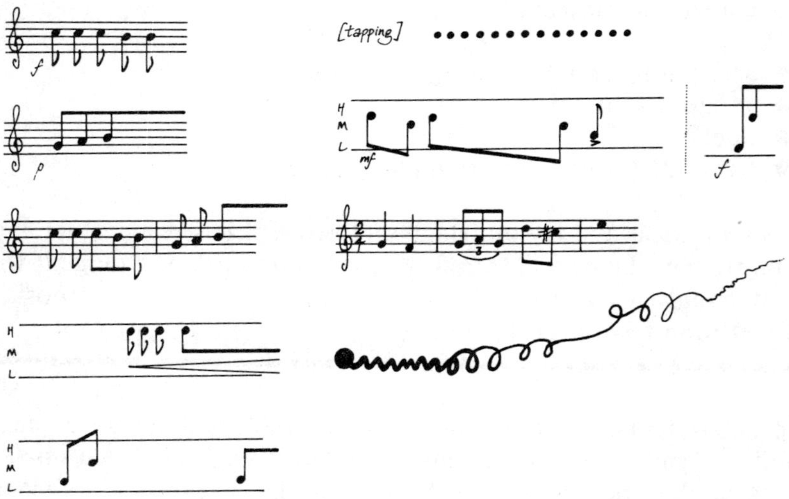

*The notation used here is explained on page 72. H, M, L indicate the High, Medium and Low registers within an instrument's range.

Score Board

This score contains various ideas, shapes and patterns. You may wish to discuss what each might mean before you begin, or try different interpretations as you go.

Version a Use it to make up short solo pieces. Move around from idea to idea. Think only about pitch at first; then think about volume too.
Or start by picking any one sign; then work through all the signs which you think suggest very SIMILAR sounds. For example, find all the quiet sounds or all the long sounds.
Or try to make each sound you choose as DIFFERENT as possible (in every way) from the last.

Version b Copy the score onto a board or large poster. Perhaps develop it into a beautiful painted design.
In a group follow a pointer as it is moved around by a 'conductor'. The conductor could indicate at times which players he would like to play particular sounds.

Version c Without a conductor and in a small group have everyone play freely from the score, fitting in ideas when you feel they will add to the interest of the piece. Sometimes you may like to find similar sounds which merge together (perhaps, even, all gradually moving to the same sign/sound), or at other times you may prefer to contrast with what the others are playing (like a solo against a friendly backing – or more violently).

Always keep your music simple and clear.

Chinese is read vertically! Arabic is read from right to left!

Part Two
The Apparatus

VOICES AND THINGS

Body-sounds: voices, claps, scratches, whistles, breaths, shuffles, pops! What instrument can boast such a wide range of sounds? Or take just the voice; what a range of possibilities there! Smooth round sounds, harsh nasal sounds, humming sounds, sliding sounds, speech sounds, in-tune sounds, out-of-tune sounds and many that it is difficult to write down clearly; kkkk, pch, dzzzz, water-down-the-plug-hole, and so on. And clapping – the part of the body you hit; whether the muscles are tensed, the part of the hand you use; all affect the pitch, volume and timbre of the sound. (If you are in a large group, each person can find a different clapping sound. Listen round the group; shutting your eyes will help concentration.)

Similar investigations and experiments can be made with breathing sounds, stroking sounds and so on. Whisper, whisper as loudly as possible, sing normally, sing lower than ever before, and higher, quieter, louder; change the shape of your lips, the position of your tongue, the shape of the mouth cavity. Try *vibrato* effects and different attacks. Strangle a sound. Concentrate on every detail.

Imitate other people's voices. Visit a zoo and imitate the inmates (use tape recordings of you and them). Sing a duet with one of them. Teach a bird to talk. Discover the secrets of ventriloquism; deceive someone.

You may now know your own voice and ability better than before. You may have found that you can sing better (or worse) than you thought. You may have discovered that there are various styles of singing and types of voice and tried some of them (*coloratura*, lyric, scat, blues, *bel canto*, croon, folk, *sprechgesang*, *falsetto*, and so on). Try to listen to experts in as many styles as possible. Compare the amounts of vibrato in different people's voices (are there differences with age, sex, . . .?); try to imitate all you hear.

There are so many types of sounds that we have a massive reservoir to use in our music. Have fun playing around with them and becoming familiar with them. Use them in a group as well as alone. The effect is often totally different. Then you will be able to select the best styles and effects when you need them from time to time in your more serious compositions. Or choose a type of sound which particularly interests you and make a piece which emphasises it.

Try to make a piece which places side by side or even superimposes the various singing styles mentioned above. The striking contrasts between jazz and operatic styles, for instance, would emphasise the character of each. It may also be an amusing piece.

Find out about Concrete Poetry. Perform some alone, with friends, just vocally, with instruments. . . . .

Extend your voice with a kazoo. Project, distort your voice through a megaphone. Ask a pianist to hold down the sustaining pedal of a (preferably grand) piano so that all the strings are free to vibrate. Sing or shout close to the strings. Listen to them vibrate in sympathy. Decide when the pedal should be raised. The piano can, of course, be used as a resonator in this way with instruments too; brass instruments are especially effective.

PIANOS AND ORGANS AND THINGS

Electronic keyboards

There is a variety of new keyboard instruments, and these are generally more portable than their older counterparts were. The electric organ, electric piano and the synthesiser are the most common. Among these the range of specifications available is so great that, if you are able to use one, you must investigate its own capabilities, special gadgets, effects, and gimmicks yourself. Briefly they all produce their sounds by electronic circuitry; each key is really an on/off switch for its own circuit which includes an oscillator able to produce the pitch required. The variety of attack, decay, timbre, and volume are all fixed directly by the designer, or by the performer setting additional switches and knobs.

Wind keyboards

The largest wind instrument is undoubtedly the pipe organ, but do not ignore its more modest relations; you may be able to use a harmonium, an accordion or a melodica. All have similar characteristics, the main one being that the sound will carry on as long as the keys are held down and the wind continues to blow (unlike the piano whose sound dies away in a few seconds). This SUSTAINING ability is useful, for it enables sounds to be held and experienced for a long time, even hours if you wish. Clusters of nearby notes are particularly effective when held; try clusters of different width and at different parts of the keyboard (if you use a ruler or longer piece of wood very wide clusters are possible); vary the volume during the time too. If you wish to use sustained sounds as a background drone it may be useful to make small wedges to fit gently but firmly between the keys; this holds them down and frees the player to do other things on the same or some other instrument.

String keyboards

You may need to take out insurance before the proud owner of a harpsichord, clavichord or spinet will allow you to be too adventurous. These expensive copies of early keyboard instruments are both beautiful and delicate; they would not stand up well to the treatment suggested for the piano, though the sounds would be fascinating. Notice the different characteristics of all these instruments (and very early pianos); their tone-colour, types of attack and period of decay. Compare the period of decay of notes at the extremes of all string keyboards.

The harpsichord has been used by many composers during this century but usually in a fairly conventional way. The piano, however, has been found to be extremely useful and versatile for the contemporary musician, for apart from the normal keyboard sounds (most instruments sound good when played 'properly') there are several other techniques you should listen to and maybe use. John Cage, a highly original American composer, has realised that objects (screws, rubbers, Plasticine, wood) placed between the strings, produce a fascinating variety of new timbres. This is easiest with a grand piano but still possible in a limited way with an upright. When the piano has been 'PREPARED' in this way it is important to play the correct keys to achieve the timbre you want, but with care a range of percussive sounds can be controlled by just one performer. The 'unprepared' notes can of course be used too.

If you can find an old upright piano which is due for the graveyard it is well worth removing the front panels and the 'action' (inside mechanism) so that only the strings are left. They can be stroked, hit, prepared, shouted at and plucked like a harp. If you need to remember particular pitches they can be labelled at the top with small adhesive labels. It is possible of course to dismantle your 'best' piano each time you want to play like this, but perhaps not too kind to its mechanical health.

Less drastic treatments can be made without dismantling or altering the instrument at all (always try, where appropriate, both with and without the sustaining – right hand – pedal):

- *glissandi* on black notes or white notes – or both simultaneously, perhaps in opposite directions (*Glissando*: sliding from one sound to another. On a keyboard instrument run your thumb nail along it so that all the pitches play rapidly one after another.)

- harmonics – silently press down notes in the middle range of the keyboard; sharply play a lower note and the harmonics of that note will start the held notes vibrating in sympathy (find out about the 'harmonic series')

- tap the case and soundboard in various places

- press the sustaining pedal down sharply; listen to the reverberations

- use beaters of various weights and materials on the strings

- use other 'beaters', finger tips/nails, coins, card, etc.

- pluck the strings (fingers, plectrums, etc.); pluck between the bridge and the tuning nut

- scrape something like a coin *along* the coiled bass strings; press very hard, vary the speed

- make cluster beaters and cluster dampers capable of dealing with a whole group of strings at once (dampers: foam-padded strips of wood the right length to fit between the parts of the iron frame)

- drop/roll ping pong balls (or other light objects large enough not to pass between the strings) onto the strings

- 'cup glissando' – beautiful but needing care – tilt an inverted cup to about 45°, press the rim firmly onto the strings of one pitch, strike and hold the key for that pitch, slide the cup along the string; the cup acts as a resonator

Play simple modern pieces to give yourself ideas, such as Howard Skempton's *Piano Pieces* (Faber, 1974), Eric Urbanner's *Eleven Bagatelles* (Universal Edition), John Cage's *Suite for toy piano* (Peters, 1960) and his *Prelude for Meditation* for prepared piano (Peters, 1960). You may also enjoy trying to perform with a singer Cage's gentle piece *The Wonderful Widow of Eighteen Springs* (Peters) which uses the sounds of a grand piano with the lid closed, or use his ideas in a piece of your own.

The other keyboard instruments are not so well supplied with easy modern pieces. The world is waiting for you to write some.

RECORDERS AND THINGS

The recorder was a very common instrument about 200 years ago but then fell out of use. Now more and more people, professional and amateur, are becoming interested in the real sounds of Baroque and earlier instruments, and recorders have become plentiful and fairly inexpensive. Some modern plastic ones are just as good or even better than wooden ones at the same price.

Though most beginners learn to play on the *descant* recorder, the other sizes, one smaller *(sopranino)* and three larger *(treble, tenor, bass)*, add tremendously to the scope of a recorder group and to the range of timbre available to a single player, from the smooth richness of the bass to the shrill insistence of the sopranino. By using the sizes best suited to a piece of music your performance can be much more effective and satisfying.

It is sometimes claimed by the unmusical that recorders are very boring instruments because the dynamic range which can be expected of them is fairly small. This is one reason why the recorder was replaced in orchestras during the eighteenth century by the transverse flute which can play much louder without going out of tune or squeaking. They are also said to be limited in the range of timbres they can produce. But the recorder is by no means boring; apart from its normal beautiful tone it has many other sounds which can be discovered and explored (some are suggested below). So far they may have been seldom used, and may have been thought of as unmusical noises to earlier composers, but they are of interest to us today.

The recorder was well-suited to Renaissance music. Though timbre and precise instrumentation are usually thought of as incidental (much early music might have been performed equally well by voices, viols, recorders, or mixed consorts) the thinness and simplicity of the recorder's timbre were ideal for early music which was primarily melodic rather than chordal. The thinness of timbre helped each melodic strand to be clearly heard and composers wrote knowing well the sort of instrumental sounds that were available. Composers (including us) writing music for the recorder today must approach it in the same way, accepting its uniqueness, its possibilities and limitations, and its range of sounds which in many cases no other instrument can produce so well. Don't use it to produce music which does not suit its character. There was no place for recorders in the intense grandeur of Brahms or the showy fire of Liszt. Perhaps after its ninteenth-century recession the recorder can now begin to justify its own place in the language and atmosphere of modern music. It's up to you . . .

Other simple woodwind instruments, very similar to the recorder, include the 'Tin Whistle' (flageolet), older than the recorder and used often in folk music; it's not hard to play the basic range of notes, though the complicated decorations and trills folk players use will need more work. The swannee whistle, with a slide like a trombone instead of finger holes for altering the pitch, is a natural clown but can with care be used to produce delicate and sincere music as well. The pan-pipes may well be the very oldest wind instrument; they have a separate pipe for each pitch and are used with amazing dexterity by folk musicians in some countries. You will not get every possible recorder sound from all of these instruments but each is useful for its own characteristics, its timbre and the sort of tune shapes which can be played on it. Try to get to know them all.

New recorder sounds:

- blow intentionally sharp or flat (try more than one player doing this simultaneously) practise doing this accurately by playing 'Wobblata' (page 54)

- blow extra hard (any high overtone), extra soft (just beginning to sound)

- vary wind pressure to make a *vibrato*; or pat your chest

- sing while blowing; try singing the note you are playing or sing it very slightly sharp or flat (to produce 'beats'), or sing a completely different tune, and so on

- close fipple, blowing hard

- close/unclose fipple while playing

- tap your fingers sharply onto the holes as if playing but don't blow

- tap the body of the instrument, for example with your finger-nails

- slide your fingers over the holes to make *glissando*

- flutter-tongue (roll an 'r' as you blow)

- mouthpiece section only : close then gradually open the end making a *glissando*; or use your finger as a slide in the end, like a swannee whistle

- mouthpiece section only : tap the open end on the palm of your hand

> Write a 'Duet for Recorder and Taped Recorder'

> Listen to the records *The Art of the Recorder* by David Munrow
>
> Play George Self's *Shriek* for 4, 8 or more descant recorders (Universal Edition)
>
> Play David Bedford's *It's easier than it looks* for 8 descant recorders (Universal Edition)
>
> Listen to / look at the score / play Luciano Berio's *Gesti* for treble recorder (Universal Edition)
>
> Go and listen to real folk musicians.

Players of orchestral or band instruments are lucky; most of these instruments have earned their popularity and place in their group because they are so versatile and useful. The possible ranges of expression and pitch means that they can be used to play many kinds of music. If you play one you have a very useful piece of musical apparatus to use in your general music-making, but don't believe that just because you play the violin, the alto sax, or the bass trombone you are more valuable to your group than the person with the recorder or autoharp or voice. It's the player that counts; if you are lucky enough to play an orchestral or band instrument make certain you do it very well and that you play it with the amount of sensitivity and real musicality it deserves. Earn your reputation as a fantastic musician, not as a thoughtless, even if skilful, mechanic.

For the last thirty years composers have demanded more and more that orchestral players make unusual sounds. Perhaps understandably, some players are reluctant – as they see it – to misuse their instruments. Using the wood side of a bow, rattling keys, singing into an instrument and so on were clearly not part of the designers' plans. But don't be sentimental; we have an instrument, a tool, capable of producing a range of sounds which can be used musically. What real musician could reject an interesting and expressive sound just because it is produced in a slightly unusual way? If a composer wants a particular sound and it can be made in that particular way, let's make it!

Listen carefully to pieces of contemporary music which use YOUR instrument and you will gradually build up a memory of the sounds you can make. Luciano Berio for instance has over some years written a set of *Sequenzas*, each exploring a particular solo instrument. They are very difficult to play but well worth listening to and studying. (Sequenza 1:Flute, 2:Harp, 3:Female voice, 4:Piano 5:Trombone, 6:Viola, 7:Oboe — (Universal Edition))

Ideas which are now familiar to many string players include playing with the wood side of the bow *(col legno)*, tapping the belly (and tapping the music stand with the bow), playing behind the bridge, using *pizzicato* but lifting up the string so it hits the fingerboard, and playing pitches in between the normal notes (microtones). Guitar players can produce some of these sounds too, in addition to strumming in various ways. Woodwind players are discovering new fingerings by which chords (multiphonics) can be produced (this is quite advanced and calls for learning new fingerings, but you have probably come across some of the sounds by accident!). They may also rattle the keys or hit them down percussively without blowing, and so on (see the list of recorder sounds on page 47, for further ideas). Brass players can make effects by rattling the valves (with or without blowing), tapping the instrument with various objects, tapping the mouthpiece (gently or you'll get it stuck), using a variety of mutes, fitting in various woodwind mouthpieces and using the grand piano as a resonator (see page 43). Some advanced players can even produce multiphonics by making parts of their lips vibrate at two different speeds, but similar sounds can be made more easily by singing into the mouthpiece while playing and producing various distorted two-note chords. If you do this but sing very slightly out of tune with the note you play the two pitches will react to give a 'beat' effect.

THE CONCRETE PATH

A composer of concrete music *(musique concrète)* uses recorded 'real' sounds, rather than pure electronically made sounds, to build up a piece of music. Sometimes they may be obviously musical (for example a violin A, a cymbal roll, a bit of Mozart), and sometimes they are 'environmental' or noise sounds (for example a tap dripping, a tree creaking, a diesel train hooting). He then combines and alters the tapes to make an interesting piece. The range of sounds he can use is infinite; it is similar to writing for a completely new sort of orchestra with new timbres and textures to listen to and play with.

Pure electronic music uses electronically-made sounds (from oscillators and synthesisers, which can be expensive) but the composer treats them and builds them up in much the same way. These types of electronic music and concrete music can, of course, never be performed 'live'; they only exist on tape exactly as they were designed by the composer and they must be 'performed' by the tape recorder in that version.

But live electronic music can be made by using electronic gadgets to modify the sounds of the instruments at the time of performance. Reverberation units, ring modulators, fuzz boxes, wah-wah pedals, filters and so on are all easily available, particularly because pop groups now use them so much. Most of them can be bought for the price of a good radio or cassette tape recorder. Instruments (and other sound sources too, such as pieces of glass, pieces of machinery, walls, floors, and humans) can all be fed through electronic changing devices. Some of them can be wired in directly (for example the electric guitar and electric piano) but most of them will need a microphone; in either case the sounds of the guitar, violin, gong or voice are at least amplified and possibly distorted as well. Two types of microphone may be used: the normal acoustic mic placed somewhere nearby – try different distances – and the contact mic, a fairly inexpensive item, which fits straight onto an instrument and picks up every small sound very clearly.

Live music can be made using a tape (either from environmental sounds such as a tap dripping or a volcano erupting, or musical sounds from your instruments or from records) and performing live with the tape as if it were another member of the group. You may like to WRITE a live part which you think will fit, or you may use the tape as an 'aural score'. Listen carefully and let the tape give you all the ideas about what to do. Pure electronic music or concrete music may be called dead. It is a sad name because it often sounds extremely exciting. But it is dead in the sense that no live performers are involved. In all types of live electronic music the audience sees the performers playing and, possibly because there is always a chance that someone will make a mistake (it keeps you tense and interested) or that someone will play a tune especially beautifully today or produce fantastic new ideas in the improvised parts, it makes the performance a more exciting experience. Do you agree? Listen to music of all types before deciding.

Part Three
Bits and Pieces

PIECES OF MUSIC

When does an improvisation become a 'real piece'? This book asks you to improvise a lot, from short melodies and single textures to complete ideas which are certainly 'pieces' of music with shape and atmosphere. The plans or recipes are printed for you, but *you* compose the pieces, which are real pieces. There are also other plans – 'pieces' – worked out in more detail, but you, the performers, are still very important. Without you the music will not really exist; it will remain a recipe for a piece, only dots on paper.

It sometimes happens that players have passed many exams on their instrument, have good 'technique' and are able to play extremely complicated and impressive music, yet they remain computers, only able to reproduce the dots they see on the paper. They would be quite lost if they were asked to play a little piece of their own. When you play a piece written down by a composer he is inviting you to join him in the making of the music; in fact in several pieces here you are actually asked to improvise sections. Just as the soloist in an eighteenth century concerto improvised the 'cadenza', you help to complete the composition and make it yours.

As you work at some of these pieces they may give you ideas for composing pieces of your own. If you have friends who play other instruments, think of ways of involving them. Learn how well they can play, the sort of things their instruments can do and the sorts of sounds they can make.

MONODY

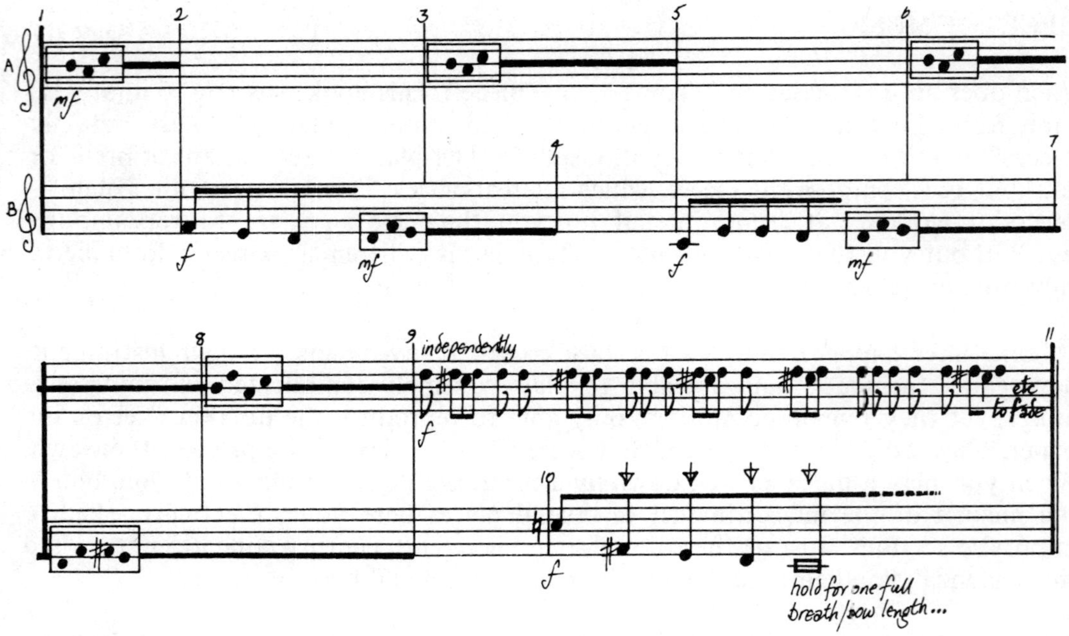

Chorale

for two groups of similar or mixed instruments *

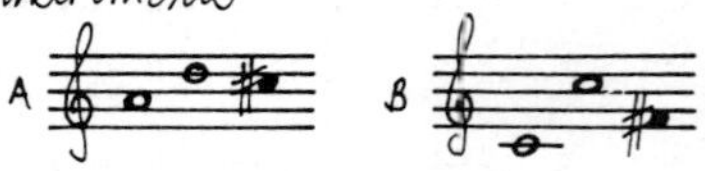

the 'boxed' improvised textures should be played staccato and remain transparent, while the unison 'chorale' episodes in part B should be sturdy ⟶ so around 8 players to each part may be ideal ⟶ alternatively part B may be played solo

* a vocal group with suitable words or other vocal sounds could be added to sing the 'chorale' ⟶ be sure you understand the atmosphere of the piece first

* a solo piano version is easily made ⟶ e.g. part A : right hand, one or two octaves higher than written ~ part B : left hand, boxed textures at written pitch, 'chorale' two octaves lower

make a more extended piece along these lines if you wish ⟶ be careful :
how much similarity? how much contrast?

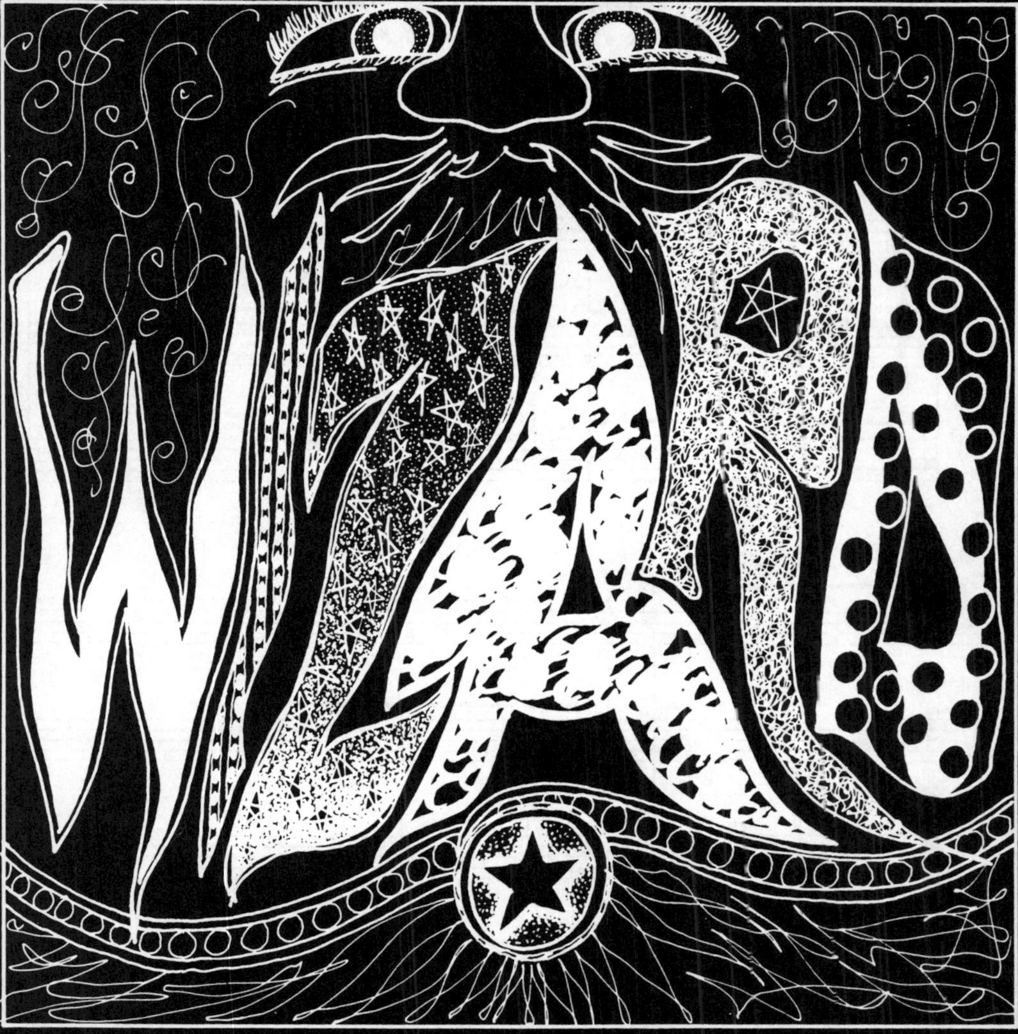
WIZARD

wobblata

this piece centres on the careful tuning of a G-major chord which comes and goes ~ indicates exaggerated vibrato and ↗ glissando to or from the written pitch ~ decide on your own way of playing the final sound ~ it should use a fresh timbre and be fleeting and delicate ~ the dynamics used in the rest of the piece are left to the conductor

1
warmth
slow
legato
melody

2
points

space
to
fill

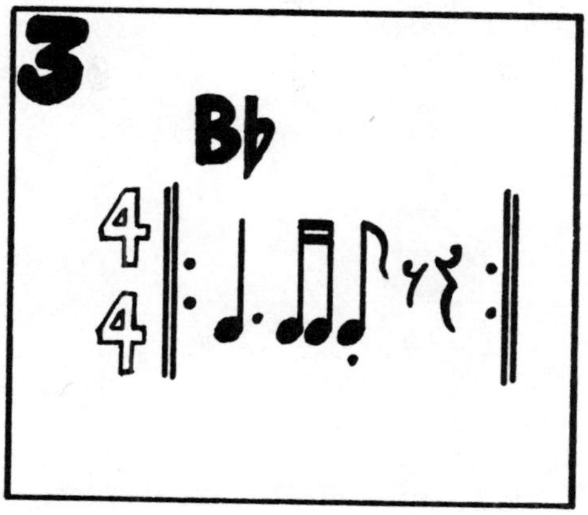
3
B♭
4
4

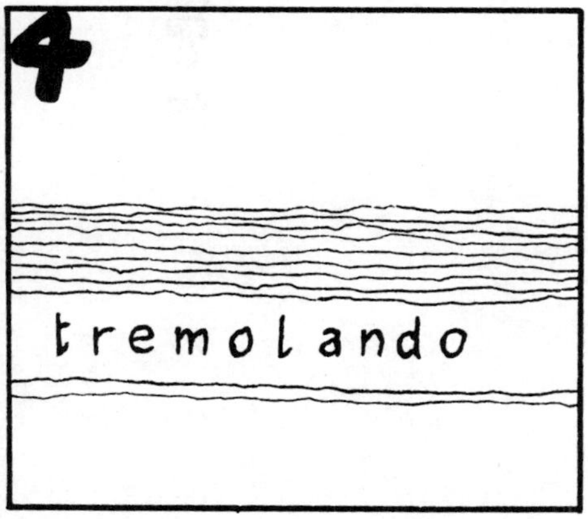
4
tremolando

5
aggro
intricate
irregular

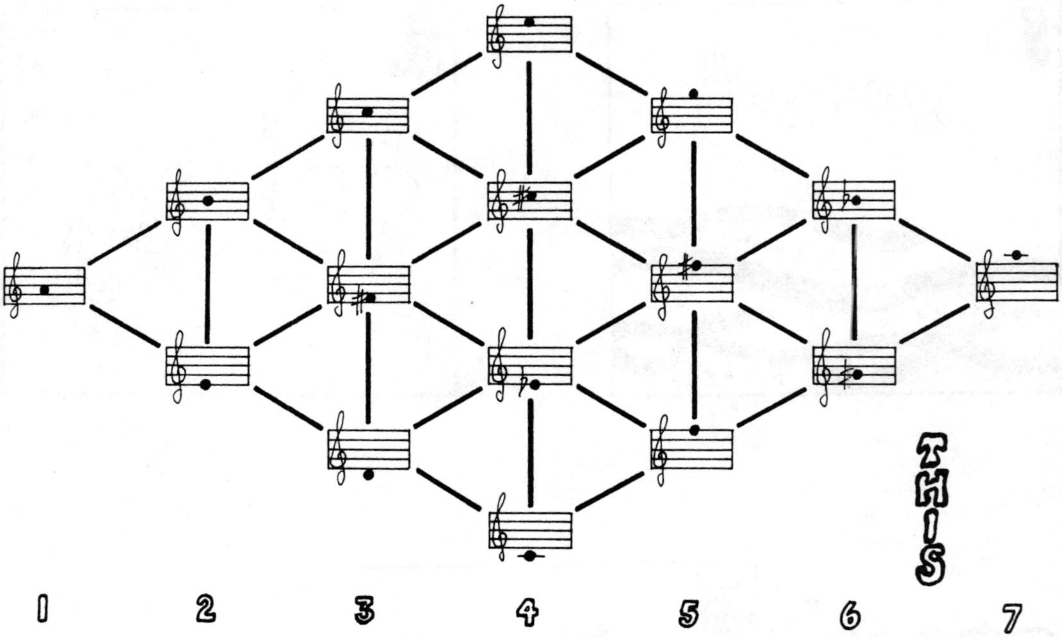

THIS WAY OR THATS

This may be played in many ways according to your imagination and ability
A beginner may write a completely new piece along these lines using only the notes he knows

Compose your own rules for using the given material ~ here are some possibilities ~ invent more

1 Make interesting seven-note melodies by moving by any route from column 1 to column 7 ~ think of rhythms, dynamics, etc. as well as the pitches

2 Make longer melodies by moving in any direction

3 Together, take any route from column 1 to column 7 ~

[a] just 7 conducted chords/events ~ attack, duration, reverberation, length of subsequent silence?
perhaps go on to repeat the process by covering the journey from 1 to 7 in six events, then in five, then four, etc.. ~ now each must choose which column(s) he will ignore each time through
chords gradually further from the original columns will happen

[b] conductor indicates 10-second periods for each column and by showing a card [or by each player having his own pack of cards] how many sounds to make in that time
perhaps indicate metrically rhythmic patterns on the cards too, in this case using 30-second periods

[c] alternatively, cards could indicate how many seconds within the period each player is to fill with his note ~ textures of different density will emerge

4 Extend any piece by moving through columns 1 to 7 to 1

5 Read columns 2 to 6 as possibilities for arpeggio movement

6 Read columns 2 to 6 as cluster ranges ~ perhaps play the written notes first, then dissolve into the cluster

7 Move gradually from chord to chord, players individually moving at different times, producing a transitional cloud effect

8 Play short repetetive figures using notes from adjacent columns ~

gradually and independently move through the columns with figures of varying length ~

9 Feel your way through intuitively ~ no plotting with other players beforehand

10 Impose an idea or title onto the above ~ RAINDROPS
TRAIN JOURNEY
TAKE-OFF
~...

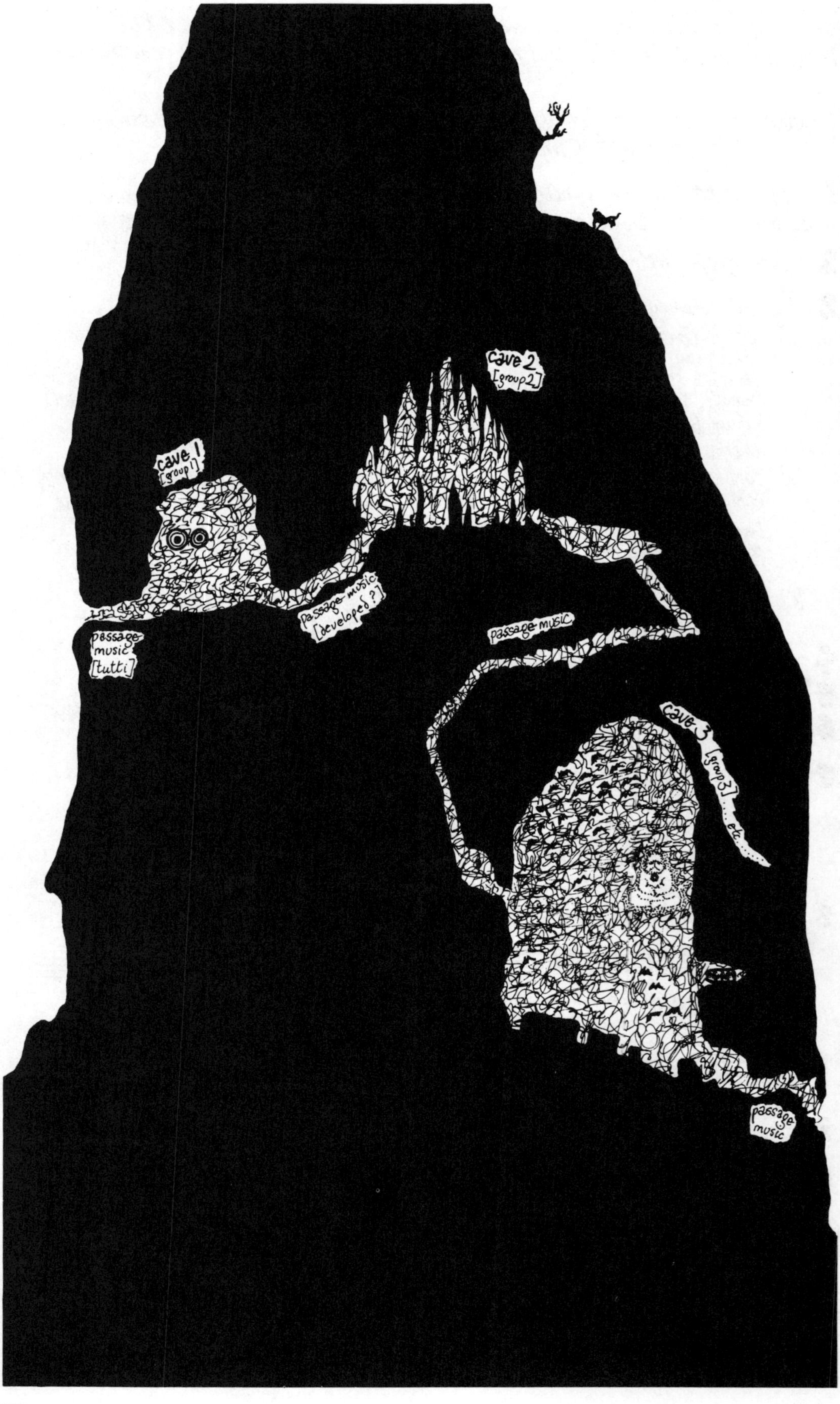
cave 1
[group 1]
cave 2
[group 2]
passage music
[developed ?]
passage music
[tutti]
passage music
cave 3
[group 3] ... etc.
passage music

HAPPENING

this piece needs no conductor → just careful ears
a group of any size or technical standard can play the piece
the initial aim is to repeat the opening sound [which needn't be prearranged] as accurately as possible ~ but mistakes may occur ~ speed may change ~ variations develop as these are incorporated into the sound other notions may occur and related variants become obvious → the first sound undergoes metamorphosis

Have you noticed how a word loses its meaning if it is repeated continuously?

machinemachinemachinemachinemachinemachine. . . . .

or try your own name

jethrojethrojethrojethrojethrojethrojethro. . . .

or those little words (quite funny words really)

whatwhatwhatwhatwhatwhatwhat. . . .

youryouryouryouryouryouryour. . . .

whowhowhowhowhowhowho. . . .

Or redivide a sentence to make

new meaningless but interesting words

newm ean ingl essbutin teres tingwo rds

EX-TEMPO-RE

time as duration

time

on time : timelag : lose
time : make time :
what time ? : keep time

egg timer : timesaver :
timetable : time signal :
common time : serving time :
up to time : time of day :
standard time : father time :
time keeper : solar time :
time limit : local time

from time to time : at the
same time : time and again :
greenwich mean time :
behind the times : time
signature : time exposure

once upon a time :
relativity

00.15	00.25	00.37	02.26	*		00.10	01.54	02.14	02.29
06.48	→	07.10	08.26	‡ ✗ ☕		07.40	08.47	08.57	09.15
06.48	→	07.10	08.30	‡ ☕	SX	08.10	09.17	09.27	09.45
07.18	07.28	07.39	08.56	A		08.40	09.47	09.57	10.15
07.48	→	08.10	09.22	‡ ✗ ☕		09.10	10.17	10.27	10.45
08.15	08.25	08.36	09.49	A	SO	09.35	10.38	→	11.02
08.48	→	09.06	10.19	A		09.40	10.43	10.53	11.11
09.18	09.28	09.39	10.54	C		10.10	11.21	11.31	11.51
09.48	09.58	10.09	11.22	B		10.40	11.47	11.57	12.17
10.18	10.28	10.39	11.58	C		11.10	12.17	12.27	12.47
10.48	→	11.06	12.24	B		11.40	12.47	12.57	13.17
11.18	11.28	11.39	12.58	A		12.10	13.17	13.27	13.47
11.48	→	12.06	13.24	A		12.40	13.47	13.57	14.17
12.18	12.28	12.39	13.58	✗ ☕		13.10	14.17	14.27	14.47
12.48	→	13.06	14.28	✗ ☕		13.40	14.47	14.57	15.17
12.48	12.58	13.09	14.28	☕		14.10	15.17	15.27	15.47
13.18	13.28	13.39	14.58	✗ ☕	SX	14.40	15.47	→	16.13
13.48	→	14.06	15.28	✗ ☕	SO	14.40	15.47	15.57	16.17
13.48	13.58	14.09	15.28	☕ b	SX	15.10	16.17	16.27	16.47
14.18	14.28	14.39	15.58	B	SX	15.40	16.43	→	17.11
14.48	14.58	15.09	16.28	C	SO	15.40	16.43	16.53	17.11
15.18	15.28	15.39	16.58	☕	SX	16.10	17.17	17.27	17.48
15.48	15.58	16.09	17.28	C	SX	16.40	17.43	→	18.11
16.18	16.28	16.39	17.55	* A	SO	16.40	17.43	17.53	18.11
16.48	16.58	17.09	18.25	* ☕ a		17.10	18.15	18.25	18.42
17.18	17.28	17.39	18.58	* A		17.40	18.44	→	19.12
17.48	17.58	18.09	19.25	* ☕		18.10	19.15	19.25	19.42
18.18	18.28	18.39	19.56	*		18.40	19.43	→	20.11
18.48	18.58	19.09	20.25	*	SX	19.10	20.13	20.23	20.42
19.18	19.28	19.39	20.52	✗ ☕		19.40	20.43	20.53	21.11
20.06	20.16	20.27	21.45	*D		20.40	21.43	21.53	22.11
20.49	20.59	21.12	22.28	*Ⓘ a		21.40	22.59	23.09	23.26
21.58	22.09	22.20	23.35	*	SX	23.10	00.33	00.44	01.01
21.58	22.09	22.20	23.44	*	SO	23.10	00.35	00.48	01.07

moment/tempo

EX-TEMPO-RE

how long has the earth existed ?	listen to the earth
what fraction of that time has man existed ?	listen to advanced mammals (chimpanzees, whales...)
	<u>the era of the silent clock :</u>
what fraction of <u>that</u> time has he measured time by the sun and moon ? [years, days, mid-day]	listen to the irregular rhythms of primitive tribal music and/or some oriental musics (how do/did they measure time ?)
what fraction of <u>that</u> time has he had instruments to measure time ? [sundial, water/sand/candle clocks...]	listen to the flowing rhythm of plainsong
what fraction of <u>that</u> time has he known how to make mechanical clocks ?	<u>for the first time time is measured by sound:</u> listen to the strict regularity of Haydn's music (not boring, but constricted within a 'tic-toc' style)
what fraction of <u>that</u> time has he measured time electronically ? [World records are now won by ·01sec ; but that's slow by computer standards...]	listen to the different feelings of time passing with Ligeti, Stockhausen, Penderecki, Berio, Cage, Terry Riley, Phil Glass, Steve Reich, Webern...
is time important any more ?	shall we soon enter the era of the **TIME MACHINE ?...**

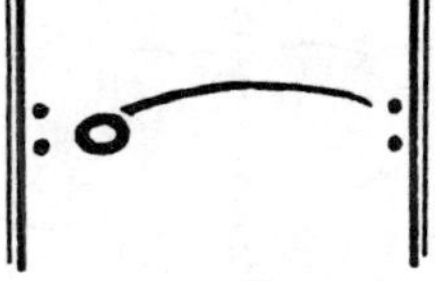

a fixed number of times

SOUND AROUND

All sorts of things make sounds. Unlike musical instruments it is as if they have sounds in them by accident.

There are two sorts of things: natural and man-made.

How do you like man's contribution to the 'World Sonata'?

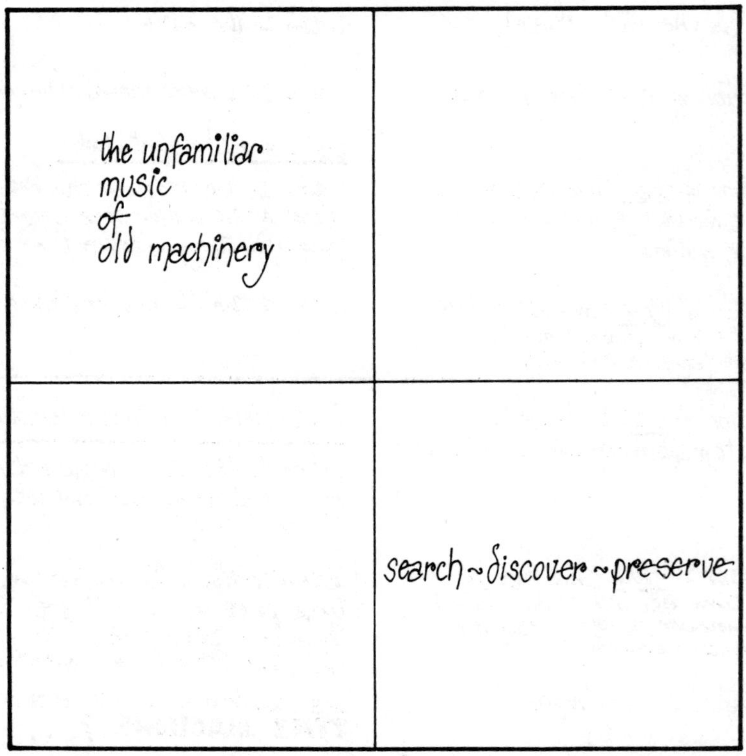

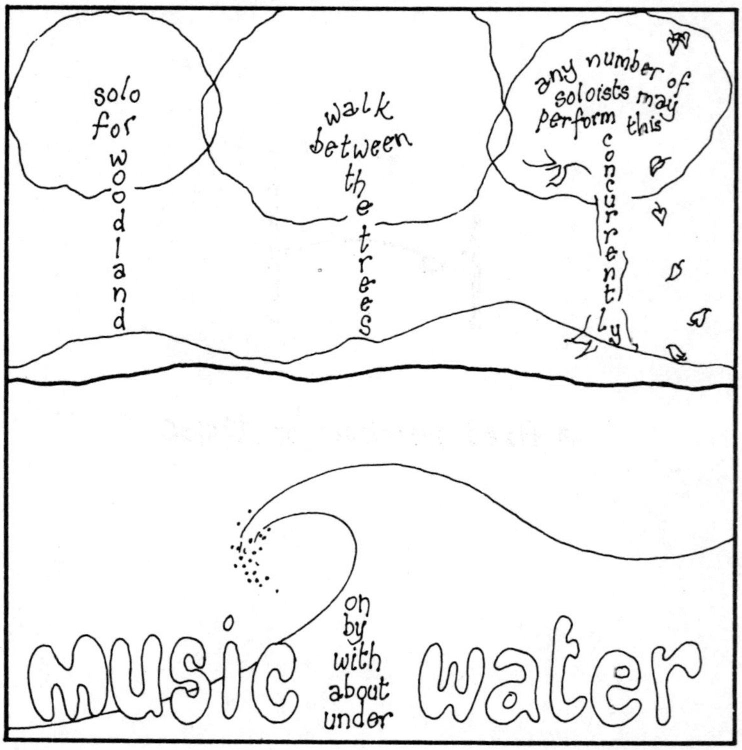

WIND MUSIC

Make wind chimes

Festoon trees and things with sonoware

Fly kites

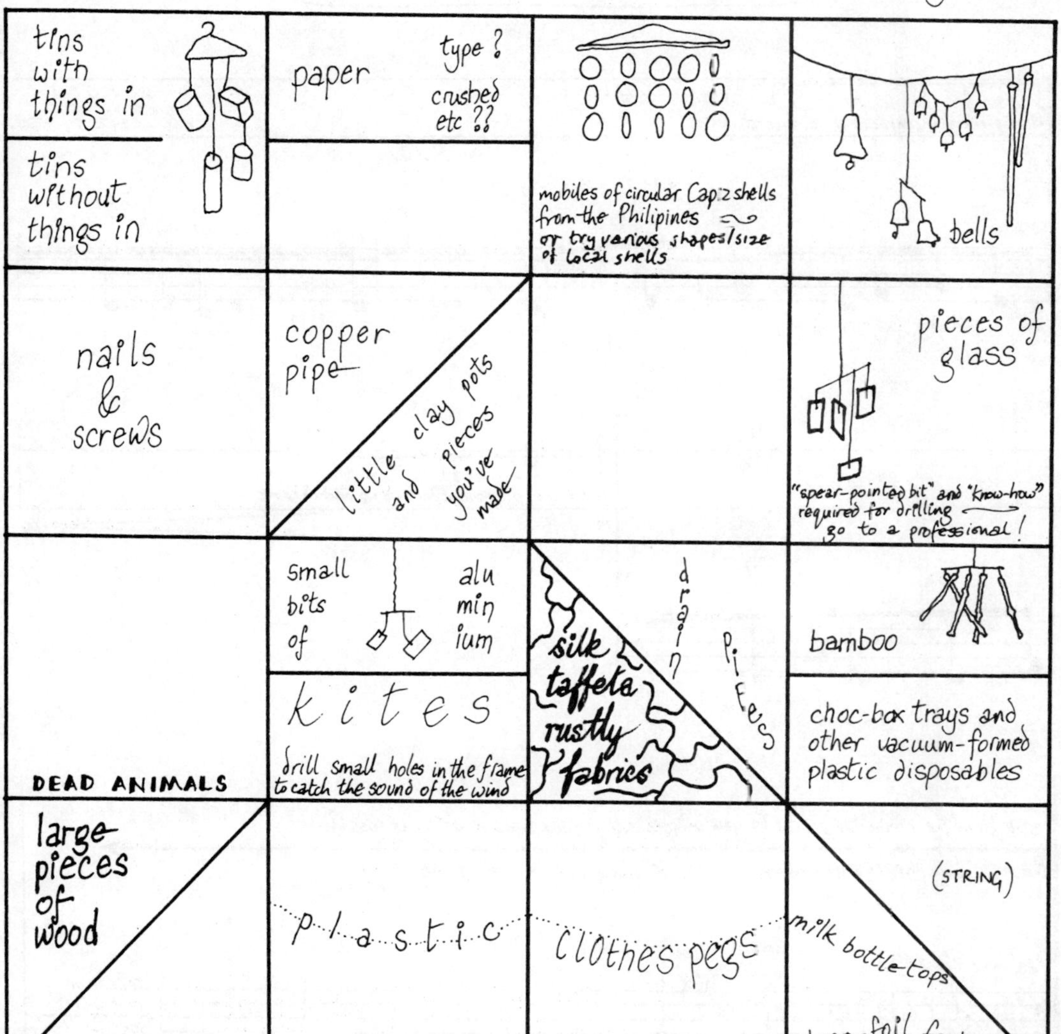

Listen to the mobiles and the sound of the wind in the other objects in earshot [trees, grass, pylons, your hair ...]

Play for longer than you listened ~ Delicate music to accompany the sounds you hear ~ they are the solo in this concerto

Listen for longer than you played

WIND CHIMES KEEP EVIL SPIRITS AT BAY.

a company

- the piece is always happy though sometimes relaxed, sometimes more excited
- the group and conductor should feel a tight identity, gently supporting the solo voice ~ arrange people spatially and visually to enhance this
- don't feel cluttered by classroom layouts ~ this is important
- the acoustic of the room is significant too ~ preferably find a friendly, clear room with clear acoustics, not dead ones

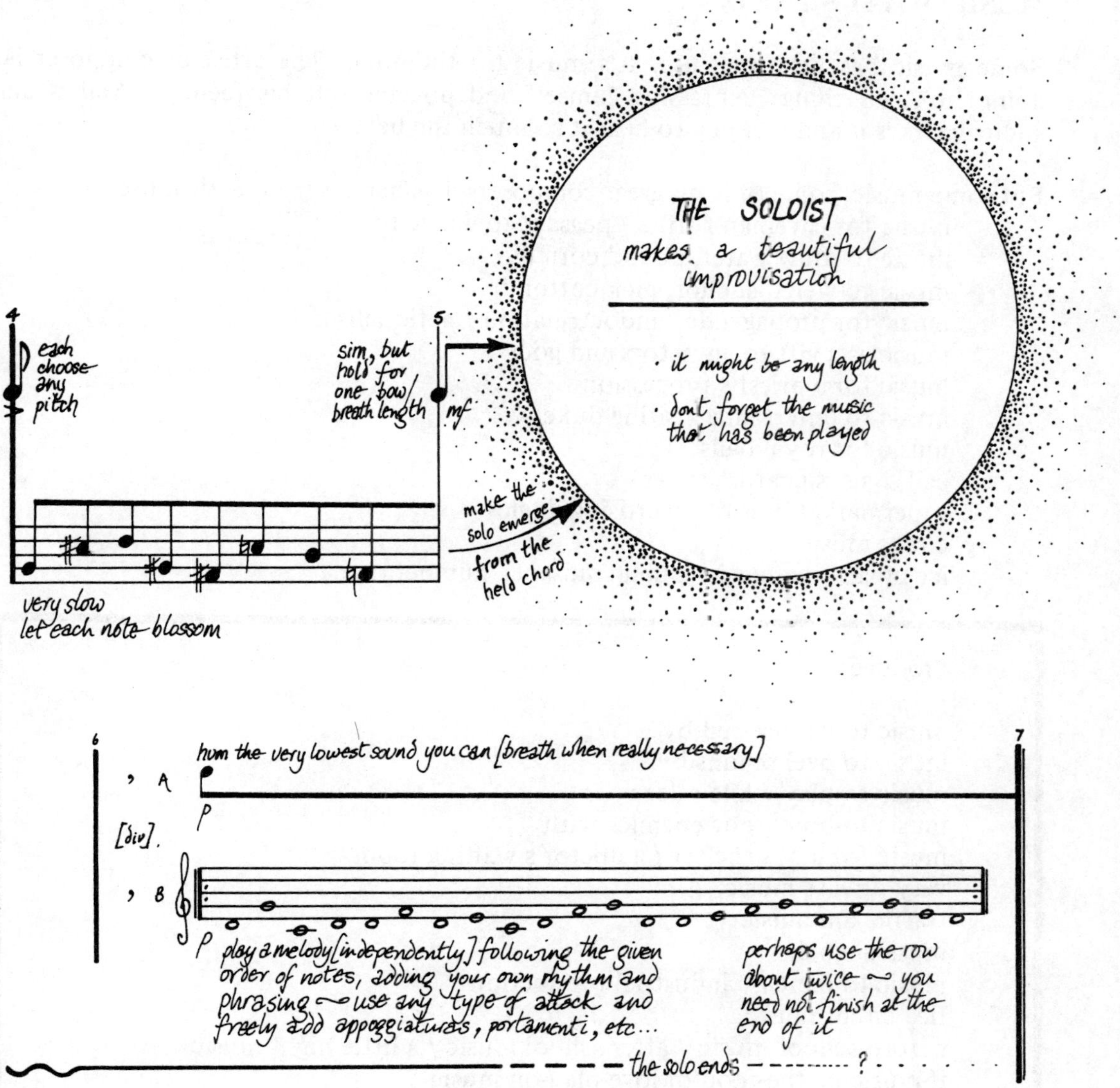

- the accompanying group needs a minimum of about 8 players — if it is a large group of mixed instruments there could be some simple orchestration of the ripieno part ~ e.g. brass : only in sections 1,4,5; guitars in 1,2,6....
- at conductor's sign 3 the soloist uses either the upper or lower line in any bar
- barlines marked with commas should be distinct breaks, but not excessively long
- the soloist may indicate to the conductor [visually or aurally] when his improvisation is drawing to a close and he wishes sign 6 to be given ~ [cp. the trill at the end of a classical cadenza]
- the soloist is not a virtuoso — nor should his improvisation try to be — clarity of ideas and execution are the goals

MUSIC: WHAT'S THE USE?

Some music has little real use. It's music for the mind. The artist or composer is doing his own thing; expressing himself and pouring out his feelings. And if an audience likes it and will pay to hear it so much the better.

But some music, some of it by great composers, has had a very practical use:

music for caveman / tribe / peasant to dance to
music to draw water, pound corn by
music to weigh anchor, pick cotton by
music for propaganda / indoctrination / nationalism
music as a gift to ancestors and gods
music for a priest's procession
music to entertain a visiting duke
music for royal balls
call signs, signature tunes
supermarket music, advertising jingles
circus music
ice cream van music (public nuisance number one!)

Produce:

music to get dressed by
music to peel onions by
music to play while asleep
music to bore your enemies with
music for a bus shelter / a doctor's waiting room
very private music
traffic jam music
musical chairs
music to increase industrial production
flea circus music
before school music / after school music / a little night music
if-music-be-the-food-of-love-play-on music

THE BIG RED FIRE ENGINE

One instrument or very small group of instruments, one player per instrument in the centre of the room

Improvise a melody [or write down some of it beforehand] following the instructions

↓ - react to the tape as you hear it

blank spaces - silent

Each bar lasts from ten to two seconds

[One conductor ad lib]

Four cassettes, four cassette recorders, four operators → in performance: volume range 1-10, blank spaces silent

→ one in each corner of the room

each tape is a continuous 10 minute recording of readings from newspapers, improvised over an unchanging rhythmic backing; make each tape different [backing, speed, source of text, topic, length of excerpts, style of speech, type of voice, type/amount of distortion...]

e.g:

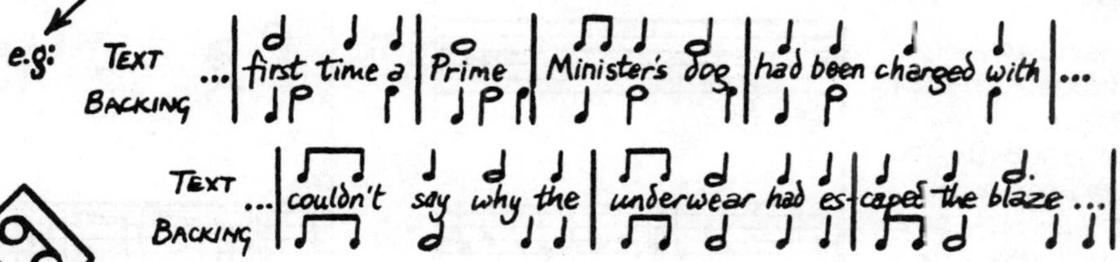

INSTRUMENT[S]	p	p	mp	↓	↓	p	mp	mf	f	ff	↙		↓	↓	↓		mf		slow mp	mp	mp	mp	fast p	
TAPE 1		5							5			2			4				4	8	9			
TAPE 2				5	1	1	1	3	3		7	2				1		1	1	1	3	1		8
TAPE 3		1	1				1	3	3			2	4			1		1	1	1	3	1		
TAPE 4				1	5			5	5	5		2		4		1		1	1	1	3	1		

		↓	↓	↓	↓	↓	↓	↓ ↙					fast p	f			slow mf			slow mf	↓	p	↓	↓	↓	fast f	mf	p	pp	ff
		10	10	10	3	1						10				5	2	1	1				3	7		2	4	6		10
						2	6	10		10		10			1	1	3		5		3	3				2	4	6	2	10
10		10						10	10	1	3				5		3	1	1				7	3		2	4			10
10	6	2		10						10			8		1	1	2	5			7				9	2				10

The Winds will

The Winds will be changeable

This is a set of variations on "Tom, he was a Piper's son", improvised by the players using the material given. It could be played by six performers, each working on one of the sections A-F, or the whole group [of any small number] could work at each section in turn. Details could be prearranged to some extent but the success of the performance will rely mainly on players listening and reacting to the music being played. There should be some reflection of the title in the piece.

The ♪ speed, which remains the same throughout, and is the same for each player, should be as fast as the players find possible. Music between double-barlines may be repeated ad lib or combined with other sections on the same line to make a longer fragment. Feel free to develop and diverge from what's written if you think it improves your version of the piece to do so.

be changeable

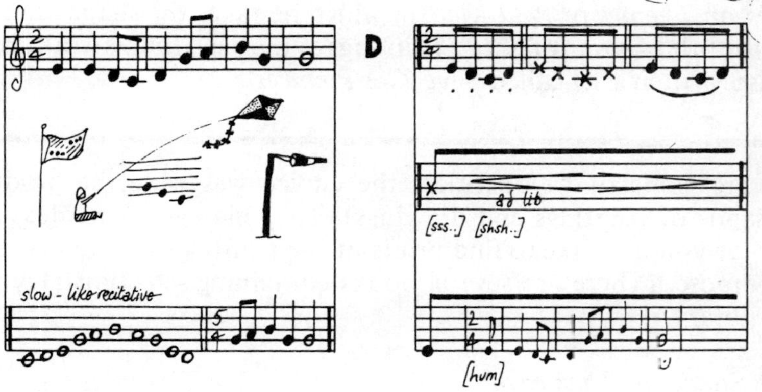

AFTER KLEE

Paul Klee (1879-1940) was a musician and poet before becoming one of the great painters of his time. Perhaps this is why his work can easily provide inspiration for musical composition; some of his paintings are clearly influenced by musical ideas. The American composer, Gunther Schuller, has written a set of instrumental pieces, *Seven Studies on Themes of Paul Klee*, in which he takes the shapes and colours, the mood or just the title of seven of Klee's paintings as the basis for his work. Peter Maxwell Davies has also written a set called *'Five Klee Pictures'*.

Here are some of Klee's titles (the choice was wide, he produced thousands of paintings and drawings). They may give you ideas right away, or you may like to find prints of the paintings before beginning to compose. (There are several books containing selections; try your local library.)

Seven Studies on Themes of Paul Klee: Gunter Schuller

Antique Harmonies
Abstract Trio
Little Blue Devil
Twittering Machine
Arab Village
An Eerie Moment
Pastorale

Five Klee Pictures: Peter Maxwell Davies

A Crusader
Oriental Garden
Twittering Machine
Stained-Glass Saint
Ad Parnassum

Other paintings

Polyphony
Fugue in Red
Scherzo with Ladder
Steps and Staircase

Kettledrummer
Black Prince
Travelling Circus

Highways and Byways
Plan of a Town
Mechanics of Part of a Town
Glass Facade

Lovesong
Embrace

Captive
Woodlouse
Woodlouse in Enclosure

Coming to Bloom
Rock Flora
Deep in the Forest
Ravaged Land

Underwater Garden
Untamed Waters
After the Flood

Hurry
Demonry
Fear
They Danced Through Fear

Rhythms
Rhythms More Rigorous and Free
Tempo of Three, Quartered

Collection of Signs
Cosmic Composition

You could make music to be played alongside the original painting. Full-size prints are sometimes available, and you may have a local picture library from which these can be borrowed. Or you could make a transparency and project it, or paint your own copy. You may like to interpret the *title* visually with your own painting, pencil design, carving and so on, and exhibit that while you play your music.

Set up an art gallery of your own work and let visitors hear your music. You could do this live if you have sufficient space, or by installing a tape recorder and earphones next to each exhibit. In this case the listeners may only 'tune in' for a short section of the piece.

Try involving poetry or sound in your musical commentary. Hold poetry and music recitals.

Write stories with background music to give them excitement, tension or tenderness. Interpret your music in movement by using puppets or getting dancers to perform in front of the painting (even in the beam of the slide projector). In this way one 'art form' will emphasise another, and will give a new interpretation to the original subject.

Move away from the concert hall, art gallery and film show situations where the audience comes to you. Instead, take your ideas outside to the passers by. Devise concerts, happenings, carnivals, street plays, and other experiences for the public. Interest them and entertain them, but don't force yourself on them or anger them.

Examples:

Arab Village – erect an Arab village

Travelling Circus – be a travelling circus

Underwater Garden – construct one in the local lake or fountain (will you have to get permission?); simulate one on land; perform a play with evocative music; devise a multi-media display

Plan of a town – draw people's attention to street art such as posters, pillar boxes and road signs. Discuss community development with them; produce a play highlighting local problems, facilities, beauty spots, and culture. Help people make their environment beautiful to look at, pleasant to hear, fresh to smell, and good to live in. Publish a community arts news-sheet with information, poems, reports, drawings, music and so on.

We're told that music (and all art) is 'fulfilling', 'uplifting', 'inspiring', 'food for the soul', 'an expression of ourselves'. Involve strangers, and your neighbours in your astounding music.

The notation

In addition to traditional notation some newer signs are used in this book.

Where there is no time signature a SPATIAL time system is used; horizontal distance on the page suggests *relative* time durations.

For example:  indicates three quick notes, a pause, a single sound, a shorter pause and two sounds not quite as fast as the first group.

The conductor gives a clear downbeat with the right hand at each numbered barline, and additional signs with the left.

For example: 

If a group is playing, all will play together at signs 1, ↓, 2, but the four sounds between 2 and 3 must be estimated by each performer so there will be overlapping. There should be no attempt to synchronise exactly here.

 short sound, but not *staccato*

 sound sustained for length of line

 the first sound is sustained and joined to the second which is short

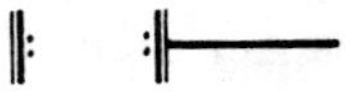 repeat figure for length of line.

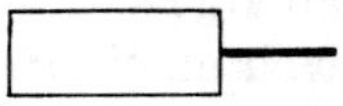 improvise on the boxed material for the length of the line.

THE LIFE C

HARPER & ROW, PUBLISHERS
London New York Philadelphia
Hagerstown San Francisco Sydney

The book was devised and produced
by Multimedia Publications Inc

General Editor: *Dr. Leonard Kristal*
Prod Mgr/Art Dir/Design: *Bob Vari*
Picture Researcher: *Judy Kristal*

First published in Holland 1980 by
Multimedia Publications Inc

Published in Great Britain by
Harper & Row Ltd, 28 Tavistock Street London WC2E 7PN

British Library Cataloguing in Publication Data
Rapoport, Rhona
Rapoport, Robert
Growing Through Life
References pg. 122–124
Includes index

ISBN 00631 81266 cased
00631 81274 paper

Colour origination: United Artists Ltd, Israel
Typeset by CCC and printed in Great Britain by
William Clowes (Beccles) Limited, Beccles and London, England